Power of the Octagon

Power of the Octagon

**Mixed Martial Arts Inspiration for
Personal and Professional Success**

ANTHONY JOHNSON

iUniverse, Inc.
Bloomington

Power of the Octagon
Mixed Martial Arts Inspiration for Personal and Professional Success

iUniverse books may be ordered through booksellers or by contacting:

iUniverse
1663 Liberty Drive
Bloomington, IN 47403
www.iuniverse.com
1-800-Authors (1-800-288-4677)

Because of the dynamic nature of the Internet, any web addresses or links contained in this book may have changed since publication and may no longer be valid. The views expressed in this work are solely those of the author and do not necessarily reflect the views of the publisher, and the publisher hereby disclaims any responsibility for them.

Any people depicted in stock imagery provided by Thinkstock are models, and such images are being used for illustrative purposes only.
Certain stock imagery © Thinkstock.

ISBN: 978-1-4620-7037-4 (sc)
ISBN: 978-1-4620-7039-8 (hc)
ISBN: 978-1-4620-7038-1 (ebk)

Printed in the United States of America

iUniverse rev. date: 12/12/2011

DEDICATION

This book is dedicated to my lovely wife, Deborah, to my children, Cory and Gabrielle, and to my parents, Gary and Frances. Without each of you, this book would not be possible.

Prologue

So what is the Power of the Octagon? In mixed martial arts (MMA), fighting cages come in various shapes and sizes. For example, Bellator events are held in a circle cage; Strikeforce uses a six sided cage; and some fight organizations still use traditional boxing rings for MMA events. The most commonly used cage design in MMA is the eight-sided Octagon, a design that is a registered trademark of Zuffa LLC (parent company for Strikeforce and Ultimate Fighting Championship). The UFC is also the entity that named the eight-sided cage the "Octagon," and today "The Octagon" is also a registered trademark under Zuffa LLC. The Octagon is a symbol for power within mixed martial arts, associated with the biggest and the best that the sport has to offer.

With that in mind, I wanted the biggest and the best to be within the DNA of this book and thus, the book is divided into eight chapters that contain the eight critical factors of success that, when deployed, will generate results. The chapters are the ingredients for achievement. You can generate results by using the advice provided in a single chapter, but when you use all eight chapters, you will become unstoppable with the force and potential to be all you are meant to be.

The sport of MMA is a sensation that has seen incredible growth and visibility during its brief existence. To help illustrate the growth of the sport, the first Ultimate Fighting Championship event (UFC 1) was held on November 12, 1993 with 2,800 fight fans witnessing the birth of a sport that would soon skyrocket in popularity. Fast forward the clock to April 30, 2011 when UFC 129 was held in Toronto, Ontario, Canada. In attendance at UFC 129 were over 55,000 fight fans, now a fractional representation of the fanatic fan base that follows all events promoting mixed martial art fights.

Even with its current popularity, MMA is still in its infancy and some of the powerhouses involved in MMA are aggressively working to build MMA to the status that the NFL and NBA currently hold in the sports world. The difference with MMA is the fan connection and level of accessibility that the sport offers compared to other major sporting organizations. Chances are that you'll never be able to go to a gym where your favorite basketball player goes and learn from the same instructors that he works with on a daily basis. In MMA, most gyms are open to fans and offer classes at extremely reasonable rates. For example, I personally have taken MMA classes at Greg Jackson's gym in Albuquerque, New Mexico, and at Ryan Bader's gym in Gilbert, Arizona. In both cases my class was less than $30.00 and even included a day pass to use their workout facilities.

Many MMA promotions offer events that allow fans to watch fighter weigh-in sessions, fighter Q&A's, pre and post-fight parties; and the UFC also hosts UFC Fan Expos on an annual basis to give fight fans access to their favorite fighters, classes, merchandise, and Q&A sessions. With other sports, you won't see the level of access that you get in MMA. Truly, it is a sport built around the fans, for the fans, and treats the fans like they are what really matters.

Another powerful, rarely discussed component of MMA rests within the sport's DNA. This component is the intense focus on achievement, accomplishment, dedication, tenacity, success, passion, and developing work practices and ethics that literally transform average people into high performance fighters.

This aspect of the sport is also one of the reasons why I am such a huge fan of MMA and why I train in MMA for purposes of fitness and knowledge. The disciplines, methods, and principles of MMA are skills and traits that can be transferred into other areas of life, be it business, academics, military, or for the purpose of becoming a highly effective person while you're between endeavors and stages of life. The skills that MMA fighters, leaders, and promoters, use on a daily basis can be used by individuals in other fields to generate incredible results. MMA fighters and trainers are some of the most dedicated and passionate athletes you'll see in any sport. For example, UFC legend Randy Couture's training coach, Neil Melanson, literally had a toe removed from his left foot in order to continue coaching.

Melanson, broke his toe during practice and the doctors told him that the procedure to repair his toe would require him to stop coaching for up to a year to let the joint properly heal. Rather than remove himself from the position for that period of time, he chose to have the toe surgically removed instead. Now that's dedication to the job. Kyle Maynard, who is discussed later in this book, is an armless and legless athlete who is working aggressively to become an MMA fighter. The examples of passion, commitment, dedication, and the drive towards excellence that are found in the world of MMA are nothing short of incredible.

This is the core concept of this book. Within these pages you will learn powerful techniques, solutions, and practices generated from the world of MMA that you can use to achieve goals, generate results, and take yourself to levels of success you previously thought not possible. When I wrote my first book, *Maximum Effectiveness*, I focused on documenting specific practices and techniques for business professionals to generate success. In this book, I wanted to write about principles of success that could be applied to a broader audience. I wanted to identify traits and solutions that a student could use to graduate at the top of his or her class. I wanted to identify skills that a sales person could use to not just make his or her sales quota, but absolutely smash the quota and earn maximum money. I wanted to document methodologies and steps that a leader could perform to take his or her company to the next level of performance and success.

Not only have I expanded the audience for who can use these ingredients for success, but all of the techniques, practices, recommendations, and methods mentioned within this book come from MMA and the people involved in the sport.

MMA is a sport with athletes who, on average, have invested years and years of training just to be a good fighter. The great fighters invest years into training and they complete daily workout tasks to hone and maintain their level of performance. When new MMA fans learn what is really involved in the sport and what the fighters have to do to become the best, they normally move from the status of occasional viewer to avid fan in record time.

I, too, went from occasional viewer to avid fan after I learned the true essence of MMA and all that is really involved in the sport. Once I got bitten by the MMA "bug" I wanted to get more and more involved in the sport. I went from fan to taking MMA classes, to working as an MMA inspector for the Indiana Gaming Commission. Working as an MMA inspector for the State of Indiana has allowed me to see different aspects of MMA that the average fan does not always get to see. I see how fighters prepare before fights. I see how fighters react to a win or loss. I see the business side of MMA, and I see the tremendous potential for enhancements that can be made to make this sport an even faster growing sensation than what it is today.

My goal with this book is threefold. First, I want to introduce people who might not be familiar with MMA to the dynamic sport that it is. If I can get just one person to start taking MMA classes or watching MMA events because of what they read in this book, then my work has been completed.

The second goal is to help promote the positive aspects of MMA. Too many people uneducated about the sport classify MMA as brutal, bloody, and barbaric. If you give it just one ounce of focus, you'll see that the sport is nothing of the sort. Yes, it's a contact sport and with every contact sport there is aggression and the potential for blood. MMA is about honor, tradition, and respect, so while you might see blood during a bout, you'll more than likely also see tremendous respect displayed by the winning fighter to his/her opponent after the bout.

Last but not least, my goal with this book is to provide the reader with practical and effective solutions, methods, and techniques that they can use to achieve great things in life, to accomplish goals, and to succeed in areas they previously thought impossible.

Thank you in advance for investing the time to read this book. May the material change you in positive and lasting ways.

Creating the Vision

"You'll never look back and regret chasing a dream. It's giving up that you look back and you regret doing." UFC Fighter, Sean Pierson(1)

DREAMS AND VISIONS

It all starts with a dream and a vision.

On January 17, 2005, Spike TV aired the season premiere of The Ultimate Fighter (TUF), and sixteen men started a journey that led them to the completion of a competition that would test them mentally and physically, but ultimately would provide them with an opportunity to fulfill a dream. The dream was to be selected as the Ultimate Fighter champion and to win a six figure contract with the Ultimate Fighting Championship (UFC) organization. The UFC, an organization owned by Zuffa LLC, headquartered in Las Vegas, Nevada, is the worldwide leader of mixed martial arts (MMA) promotions and events. The UFC is to MMA what the National Football League (NFL) is to football.

The first season of The Ultimate Fighter competition pitted man against man and sixteen fighters were whittled down to two finalists: Forrest Griffin and Stephan Bonnar. Each week an episode of TUF displayed fights that showed men giving it their all. Men doing everything possible, physically and mentally, to win, and both Griffin and Bonnar stood to dominate at the end of season.

The Ultimate Fighter season finale was held on April 9, 2005, and the fight that took place between Griffin and Bonnar was epic. Rounds one through three were a display of striking intensity that had both fighters getting their even share of strikes, as well as even number of hits. By the end of round three, both fighters were bloodied and near exhaustion and yet they both stood strong when the horn called the round to an end. This fight is credited as being one of the events in the UFC history that had a substantial impact on the overall success and fan awareness of the sport, and of the UFC organization in general. Even Dana White, UFC President, was quoted as saying this fight was the "most important fight in UFC history."(2) The fight, a battle between two dedicated and determined men, went to a decision by the judges to determine the winner. Forrest Griffin was victorious that day, but because of the heart that both men showed, both Griffin and Bonnar received six figure contracts with the UFC. Forrest went on to win the light-heavyweight belt from Quinton "Rampage" Jackson at UFC 86, and both fighters are still active and successful in the UFC today. Both Griffin and Bonnar identified, fought for, and realized their dream of being a UFC fighter.

They were in the right place to achieve their dreams, were prepared to receive the benefits of achieving their dreams, and took action to obtain their dreams.

Regardless, if your dream is to become the next world champion MMA fighter, or the CEO of a Fortune 500 company, you must have a dream, and you need to follow the vision of the dream. The great Napoleon Hill, the author of *Think and Grow Rich*, once wrote, "Cherish your visions and your dreams, as they are the children of your soul, the blueprints of your ultimate achievements."(3) I believe that every one of us is born to fulfill greatness during our time on Earth. The challenge bestowed upon us is to identify our potential and the things we truly want to achieve, as well as to properly prepare to achieve our dreams.

Finally, we need to take the necessary action to put our abilities into motion to make our dreams happen. It is too easy to ignore these steps and just live a life of basic existence. Your dreams may be much larger than mine, or vice versa, but the fact is that we all have dreams and we all were put here to achieve them.

In life, we have the opportunity to achieve our dreams or be part of someone else's accomplishments. UFC fighter, Kenny Florian, said it best: "You can't go living out someone's dream. You have to chase your passion, and chase what you love. I knew I had to do that. Otherwise, I'd be the old guy in the rocking chair saying, 'I wish I could have done that.'"(4)

Success doesn't happen without a dream and a vision, and part of the effort of achieving your dreams is to monitor your progress.

Sometimes, tracking our progress is subjective or requires us to focus on intangible results, but one of the great things about a sport like MMA is the fact that the goal and end objective is tangible and visible. Winning the championship belt is the ultimate reward for the high level of work and effort that it takes to become an MMA champion, but before winning the championship, a fighter can track his or her progress by analyzing their fight record, martial arts belt certification, and physical fitness achievements such as strength, weight, and cardiovascular goals. The same tangible results can be identified and tracked for almost any life objective you strive to achieve. Rare is the man or woman who achieves success without having the dream or vision of what they are striving for. Powerful is the force that is a vision led by fierce determination, focus, and motivation.

THE ULTIMATE OBJECTIVE

Identifying and working to realize your dreams is a brave step that many fail to take. How many stories have you heard about people who wanted to become something in life, and yet they are doing nothing to actually achieve this vision? Opera composer, Gian Carlo Menotti, once said that, "Hell begins on the day when God grants us a clear vision of all that we might have achieved, of all the gifts which we have wasted, of all that we might have done which we did not do."[5] In a later chapter, I will teach you how to fuel the motivation you need to achieve your goals and objectives, but the first step towards developing any level of success is to first understand what you want to accomplish.

World famous inventor and scientist George Washington Carver was quoted as saying, "Where there is no vision, there is no hope,"(6) and I would add that where there is no vision, there is only randomness and chance. In other words, one might achieve a degree of success just by being in the right place at the right time, but this is like playing the lottery as your only vehicle of wealth accumulation. You might win, but chances are that you won't and your efforts (and money) will just be wasted. But armed with a dream and the passion to achieve your dream, you will be unstoppable.

As mentioned previously, those who know their ultimate objective or milestone relative to achieving a dream have a greater chance of staying on course and actually getting what they are striving for in life. If you know your ultimate objective, you can reverse engineer the steps that it takes to achieve your dreams.

Reverse engineering basically means you look at your final product (or achievement, in this case) and you dismantle it; break it down into the components that were required to assemble it. Reverse engineering is also a great way to make better an existing product, and the same philosophy can be applied to your dreams. For example, let's say your ultimate goal is to be the Vice-President of Sales for a large corporation.

Armed with that target, you can then reverse engineer the steps that you have to take in order to achieve the objective, or you can reverse engineer the path taken by someone who has already achieved the goals you are working to accomplish. Below is an example of how this process might look for you.

In reviewing illustration 1.1, you'll notice that starting from the bottom of the page and moving up, you'll see the proposed steps that the individual in the example has mapped out to chart his path towards achieving the VP of Sales position. Within each milestone are details about what his selected mentor (someone who achieved what he's working to achieve) completed, as well as what he thinks he must do to not only achieve the same results, but to achieve an even greater degree of success in each applicable step of the process.

Ultimate Objective Reverse Engineering
(Modeled from mentored VP of Sales)

Illustration 1.1

| Achieve VP of Sales | Age 30. He achieved VP of Sales within two years. He drove company YOY growth by 40%. I will set a personal goal of 50% YOY growth, as well as work to win the Malcolm Baldridge quality award. |

| Assistant VP of Sales | Age 28. He was promoted as the company's youngest AVP to date. As AVP he managed 20 DM's, and 250 reps. He was instrumental in moving the company to Fortune 500 status. While he was AVP, the company grew revenues by 25% year over year (YOY). I will set personal goals of 30% YOY targets and will also work to achieve client satisfaction and national recognition for the company as a leader in our industry. |

| Regional Sales Director | Age 26. He was promoted to regional sales director within 2 years of being a DM. As RSD, he managed 5 DM's and 80 reps. His region did not hit 100% of quota the first year due to economic downturn, but he hit 105% the next year. I will set a personal quota of 110% and ensure my region has the highest margins, revenues, and client satisfaction ratings. |

| Account Executive | Age 24. He was promoted to district manager within 2 years. As DM he managed 10 reps and hit 102% of quota and achieved DM of the year recognition. I will work to hit no less than 110% of quota and will also manage my company's most strategic accounts. |

| District Sales Manager | Age 22. After college, he worked as an account exec. He achieved 100% quota from year one on. I will join a firm in my desired industry and hit 110% of quota plan. I will also bring in large new clients and drive client satisfaction to new levels. |

| College | Age 18. He graduated with a 3.8 GPA from a local university. I will go to Stanford University or Yale and graduate with a 4.0 GPA. |

You can also use the previous process to identify gaps or challenges you have to overcome. Let's say, for example, the aspiring VP in our reverse engineering sample did not graduate college, or maybe took longer to get promoted from one position to the next. Some might think that it's practically impossible for someone without a college degree to achieve the level of VP or an executive position of that caliber. This is not true, and there are hundreds and hundreds of examples where people without college degrees have moved up from within companies to hold executive positions, if not end up leading the company as CEO. Never let a perceived challenge block your desires and dreams. A person without a degree is going to have to work harder and achieve solid results in order to prove him or herself, but nothing is impossible.

The reverse engineering exercise allows people to see where they might have gaps such as this and then plan for exactly how they will overcome the challenge. Breaking down the steps that you'll need to follow in order to achieve success does not mean that you won't run into unexpected challenges, delays, or that you won't face defeats, but if you know what you're fighting for, and you know what steps to follow, your chances of success will outweigh those of the person without aim or purpose in this world.

HOW TO IDENTIFY YOUR DREAMS AND VISIONS

If you are struggling to identify your dream, or finding it difficult to create a vision, or even connect with THE thing that you were born to do, let me ask you this question.

What would you do today if you were 100% sure that you would not only succeed, but that you would be considered one of the best in the world at it?

Or better yet . . .

What would you do today that absolutely jives and excites you, if you were 100% sure that you would not only succeed, but that you would be considered one of the best in the world at it?

There's a clear difference between the two questions. There are people who are really good at business, sports, and entertainment, but they hate the very thing that is generating results for themselves. They do this thing they are really good at because it's what they are known for, or just because it pays the bills. This is not how you define your dream.

You define and create your dream by identifying the thing that absolutely excites you. The thing you love doing every day that you would be more than happy to do for the rest of your life. Maybe it's fighting in the UFC? Maybe it's traveling? Maybe it's helping people who are in need? Only you know the answer to this question, and it's critical that you answer it.

T.K.O. (Tips, Knowledge, and Objectives)

Before starting your day, make a list of what you want to accomplish during the workday and while you're at home. Get detailed with the action items and write down the expected results. For example, if I'm going to contact new clients, I'll start my daily list with things such as "Contact Bob Smith regarding new deal. Bob is excited about the offer and wants to place his order this week." I'm a firm believer that if you tell the universe that something is going to happen and if you're prepared for the situation to happen, it will happen. Write out your day in detail and make it happen!

When your dreams and visions are identified and defined, you will be unstoppable. Examples of this statement are rich within the world of MMA. All you have to do is look at some of the current UFC Hall of Famers such as Chuck Liddell. Chuck "The Iceman" Liddell is a legend within MMA. Chuck made his UFC debut in 1998, but if you ask any MMA fan to name a fighter who has had a huge impact on the sport, chances are that you're going to hear the name Chuck Liddell quite often. Other legends of the sport such as Randy Couture, Royce Gracie, Matt Hughes, Mark Coleman, Dan Severn, and Ken Shamrock are all UFC Hall of Famers, and all have deeply impacted MMA in a positive way, as well as established success and positive fight records in the UFC.

You don't get to the level of success that Randy Couture has by not having a plan, a dream, and a vision as to where you want to go in life. You don't get to a fight record of 46 wins, 9 loses, and zero draws, which is Matt Hughes' current fight statistic at the time of this writing, unless you're one dedicated and focused individual who knows what they want in life.

Thinking "big picture" about what one desires in life can be a daunting and intimidating task. For example, think about the amount of time, training, energy, and money involved in becoming a professional fighter. Most fighters are brown or black belt level practitioners in some form of martial arts, and many fighters have high level certifications in multiple disciplines. The average time involved in achieving a black belt is in the range of three to four years. Even if additional fighting techniques and sparring were included in the mix while the fighter achieved brown or black belt, you're still looking at several years just to achieve a decent level of fighting certification. Not only is there the investment of time, martial arts training, equipment, and even fighting costs money. Dojo's, or martial arts training gym's, can cost between $50 a month to hundreds of dollars a month for high-end schools. In addition to the time and money, there's the unquantifiable cost of bruises, cuts, and even broken bones.

So it's easy for someone just starting out in the sport to get overwhelmed and intimidated by the whole process if they think about it from start to finish.

With that in mind, it's important to remember that Chinese philosopher Lao-Tzu once said that, "A journey of a thousand miles begins with a single step."(7)

Don't get intimidated or overwhelmed by the long journey you must take; learn to envision the journey, chart your course, and enjoy each step of the voyage.

Professional project managers create massive project plans just to organize simple business flows such as order processing, and most people won't take the time to map out what they want to do in life, what steps they have to take in order to achieve milestones, and what the end goal might look like when they are finished. The beautiful thing is you don't even have to get that detailed with the plan. It can be as simple as:

- Month One: Find a gym, purchase basic equipment for training. Start lessons.
- Month Two: Earn yellow belt
- Month Three: Earn orange belt
- Month Four: Find a boxing camp and start taking lessons
- Month Five: Earn green belt
- Month Six: Stop boxing class and join Muay Thai class
- Month Seven: Earn blue belt
- Month Eight: Register for first amateur MMA fight

In other words, this process does not have to be complex. If you want to get detailed and plan out every week, every month, every year, that's fine, but you have to map the plan in a way that resonates with you.

In other words, begin planning your action and tracking your success. If it takes you two months versus one month to complete a stage, adjust and move on.

Life is about change and adapting.

As long as you're disciplined in your endeavors and not missing goals and milestones because of laziness, or lack of preparation, you're adapting and adjusting. I've dedicated this chapter's "Rules of the Octagon" exercise to the steps you need to take to identify and map out your dreams and the steps you need to take to achieve them.

CREATING YOUR LEGACY

Creating a vision is also about defining a legacy. Georges St-Pierre once said, "Legacy is making history in a sport, making something people will remember for a very long time, for many generations."(8) In life, there is a beginning and an end. Your legacy is what you leave behind when your ride is over. Think about business people like Henry Ford and Andrew Carnegie. These are people who achieved so much success and generated so many results during their lives that people today still know who they are, as well as respect their families. In the world of MMA, there is a family that has already established a legacy, and the family is only getting started. This family is named Gracie. The words "Brazilian Jiu-Jitsu" are synonymous with the name Gracie. Gracie Jiu-Jitsu was first established by Carlos Gracie in 1925. The Gracie family created the Ultimate Fighting Championship, and aired the very first UFC competition on November 12, 1993. This event was won by Royce Gracie, one of the most predominant and legendary fighters in UFC history.

Today, the Gracie legacy and tradition is maintained by family members such as Ryron and Rener, who educate thousands of students via their schools and training videos.

Greg Jackson and Pat Miletich are other examples of prominent figures in the world of mixed martial arts that have defined a strong legacy in the sport.

Greg Jackson is, arguably, one of the best modern day MMA coaches in the industry. Jackson's gym out of Albuquerque, New Mexico, has seen warriors the likes of Georges St. Pierre, Shane Carwin, Diego Sanchez, and Jon Jones, just to name a few. Jackson is recognized as a prominent leader by many within the industry, and has gained formal recognition in the form of accolades generated for his coaching and the effectiveness of his gyms. Jackson is known for coaching and fight strategy effectiveness, but he's also known for the amount of care and individual focus that he offers his fighters. When Jackson won the 2009 Fighters Only World Mixed Martial Arts Award for coach and gym of the year, he said, "I think the key is watching people change their lives and fulfill their dreams. Watching people get better and just watching how it can change your life and how it can better your life. Just being part of that process of helping so many people have a better life I think is really the addiction I have to it."(9)

A common theme to success in life, as with people who establish life-long legacies, is to serve others and to have the passion of helping others as one of your focus points. Author and master motivator Zig Zigler said, "You can get everything in life you want if you will just help enough other people get what they want,"(10) and this quote rings true in almost all facets of life.

Jackson established his legacy by building up a long list of champion fighters, and did so by putting people first.

Pat Miletich is another coaching and fighting legend in the sport. Pat's Miletich Fighting System was taught from his gym in Iowa, which had spawned a number of incredible fighters the likes of Matt Hughes, Mark Coleman, Tim Sylvia, Bart Palaszewski, and Jens Pulver, just to name a few. Most MMA gyms are intense and physical, but Pat's gym was known worldwide for its intensity. The gym's pace and expectations were so well known, books such as *Blood in the Cage* by L. Jon Wertheim and *The Fighter's Heart* by Sam Sheridan included detailed content about Pat and stories of his gym. Highly effective facilities, past and present, such as Pat Miletich's gym generated their results by utilizing key elements of success that you will read about in this book. The fundamental key possessed by Pat and his team was the ability to create a vision, follow it, and generate an offering that allows other people to become successful as well. This is how you create a legacy.

T.K.O. (Tips, Knowledge, and Objectives)

Find someone who is generating the level of success you want to achieve, do the things that they are doing in life, and then you'll start to eventually achieve the level of success that they currently enjoy. One of the best steps you can immediately take in order to be successful in any endeavor is to find a mentor, someone you can mirror for success. Ideally, this will be someone you can interact with on a one-to-one basis, but if not, then select someone who is the absolute best in their field. If you learn from the best, and mirror the best, you become the best.

THE STORY OF TAPOUT

When hearing names such as Skyscrape, Punkass, and Mask, one probably doesn't immediately think that these are names of owners of a multi-million dollar apparel company, but then again, the company known as Tapout is not your typical company. Formed in 1997 by Charles Lewis, Jr. (Mask), Tim Katz (Skyscrape), and Dan Caldwell (Punkass), Tapout started as an idea and a dream generated by these three individuals and their love of a new sport they had discovered called mixed martial arts. Tapout, a company that sold only four shirts during its first event, is now a company that now generates more than $200,000,000.00 in annual revenues. Its story is filled with incredible milestones.

Tapout was recently acquired by Authentic Brands Group, a company that offers the potential to take Tapout to new levels of growth and exposure. Tapout is a story of highs: three friends working together to build a successful company, as well as positively impacting a sport they all loved. It's also a story of lows such as the untimely death of Charles Lewis, Jr. (Mask) when he was involved in a car accident that took his life in 2009. Most important, Tapout is a story about dreams and the fulfillment of them. Tapout is proof that nothing is impossible if one is passionate and dedicated to achieving one's dreams and visions. A quote from Mask posted on the Tapout site summarizes this topic with incredible eloquence and passion. The quote reads:

"Life is full of influences. It's your application that sets you apart.

That's something I wrote to myself and completely believe in. You can't be scared to set out to do something in life because you believe it may be similar to something, or because you don't know the clear cut path on how you're going to accomplish your goal or dream! Just take a step towards your belief daily—fearlessly, wholeheartedly, digging and dreaming within yourself, believing that as you push on through sacrifice, you will one day stand alone on top of a hill that you created that now encourages and inspires others to chase their dream. Knowing that through tenacity and patience, anything can be achieved.

If you'll simply believe . . ." **Mask—www.tapout.com**

RULES OF THE OCTAGON

Rule #1: Know your dreams and set your vision:

Exercise—Create a written document and title it "Octagon Rule #1: My Dream and Vision." In this section, write down what your life dreams are and what you see as your vision of success in your life. In this exercise, get as detailed as possible. If you say generic things such as "I want to be rich," you'll get generic results. Remember, to a person that is starving and homeless, having $10,000 is rich. If you say you want to be rich, you must define what rich means to you and this becomes your target. Also, the more detailed you can get about simple things such as the training you achieve, the car you drive, the place where you live, your day to day life, the better this exercise will be.

I believe that life gives you exactly what you want. Personally, I believe that I've received everything that I've asked for, when the time came that what I asked for best served me. In other words, I believe that people receive things in life when it's time to receive them and when they're meant to receive them. How many times have you heard stories about people who achieved a degree of success, won a large sum of money, or received a big promotion only to fail, lose everything, and eventually end up with less than they started with?

This is life's little way of teaching lessons and sometimes the only way to learn something is the hard way.

True success is generated when one plans out his or her life and prepares for success, expects success, and does whatever it takes to ethically and honestly deserve and earn success.

Here's an important thing to remember about your dream and vision story. Ideally, you want to keep this document to yourself, or only share it with the people you hold closest to your heart. An unfortunate thing about human nature is that many people like to break down other people and accidentally (many times, on purpose) kill dreams. Imagine how you would feel if you wanted to be a doctor and after reading your dream and vision story, your "best friend" said something like, "You, a doctor? Dude, there's no way you'd ever become a doctor. You're way too dumb!" Even if your friend was joking, this impacts you, and maybe it's conscious or subconscious, but you will start to doubt yourself. Fear, doubt, and lack of confidence are the killers of dreams and visions. Show your dream and vision story only to people you completely trust. Also, if anyone ever shares their dreams and aspirations with you, always be cognizant of how you treat this opportunity, as well as what you tell the person after reading or hearing his or her aspirations. That person is sharing something personal with you, so listen to them, encourage them, and offer to help them achieve their dreams and goals any way that you can. This is how you impact people in a positive and resounding way.

It is critical that YOU create the dream and vision story. Only you truly know what real success means to you, and this is why you must document it and keep it visible. People have a way of subconsciously programming other people, so you need to be aware of this and stick to YOUR dreams. Have you ever had an experience where you were having a good day and then you walked up to someone having a crappy day? All of a sudden this person starts saying things about how his or her day sucks and then they start to get you believing the same thing. It's social conditioning and basically how we create interpersonal congruency with each other, but it can also be a negative thing. When I'm talking with someone and they go on about how poorly their day is going, I tell them I hope it gets better for them, and that my day has been awesome. Your dreams and visions are the same way. You might be talking with a peer or someone working to achieve the same things as you in life, and they might stress the importance to achieving what they define as success. If someone tells you that driving a new Mercedes is THE way of knowing you've achieved success, you might just fall for it. If owning a Mercedes is not important, and just living a debt-free life is a goal, don't fall for others' dreams. Tell them that you hope they achieve their life dreams and that you're working to achieve yours.

Once your dream and vision story has been documented, place it in a location where it will always be handy, and then read it often.

Outline your desired accomplishments in bullet form, and remember that what you document has to resonate with you.

An example of how to document your dreams and visions in bullet form would look as such:

- Complete college degree with 3.8 GPA or higher

- Start my own corporation. MMA fighter marketing and management
- Achieve black belt in Tae Kwon Do within three years
- Generate the following income:
  - 2011—$150,000
  - 2012—$185,000
  - 2013-$200,000
  - 2014-$250,000
  - 2015-$300,000
- Purchase new home. five bedrooms, pool, one acre of land, entertainment room, four car garage, basement
- Open my first MMA gym. Open total of three gyms by 2015
- Achieve liquid wealth targets of :
  - 2011-$250,000
  - 2012—$300,000
  - 2013-$500,000
  - 2014—$750,000
  - 2015-$1,000,000
- Establish a healthy relationship with a person that will be my life partner
- Donate 10% of my annual income to charity and local efforts that I want to support

Obviously, the goals would change depending on what you're looking to achieve. If your dream is to become a doctor, your objectives will look totally different than those of someone looking to become a pro athlete, but the point to stress here is that you need to add as much detail to your bullets as possible.

If you can associate timelines to your dreams and visions, this will be even more effective. I'm a believer that things happen in the timeframe in which they are supposed to happen, but it's good to monitor your progress against the timeline you estimated for the completion of your goal.

Always remember, if you know what you're looking to achieve in life, and if you fight for these dreams and your visions of greatness and excellence, you will achieve everything you've set yourself up to achieve. If your dreams include achieving large goals and objectives, as well as defining and establishing a legacy in the process, just think about the life you will live.

THE SCORECARD

- DOCUMENT YOUR DREAMS AND VISIONS
- UNDERSTAND THAT YOU ONLY HAVE ONE LIFE TO LIVE AND WHAT YOU DON'T ACCOMPLISH NOW WILL BE IMPOSSIBLE TO ACCOMPLISH IF YOU'RE WAITING FOR THE PERFECT TIME AND PERFECT SITUATION
- SUCCESS DOES NOT HAPPEN WITHOUT DREAMS AND VISIONS
- KNOW THAT WHAT YOU PUT YOUR HEART AND MIND INTO, YOU WILL ACCOMPLISH
- START BUILDING YOUR LEGACY TODAY
- ROADMAP YOUR GOALS, OBJECTIVES, DREAMS, AND VISIONS AND KNOW WHERE YOU'RE GOING IN LIFE
- FIND SOMEONE WHO HAS WHAT YOU WANT AND DO WHAT THEY DO TO GENERATE THE SAME RESULTS
- DON'T STOP UNTIL YOU GET WHAT YOU WANT

Chapter 2

Knowing What's at Stake

"With hard work, dedication, and sacrifice comes reward." Tito Ortiz, Ultimate MMA Magazine, June 2010

UNDERSTANDING YOUR "WHY"

Now that you understand what it is that you're going after, it's critical that you understand why you're going after it, as well as what's at stake if you achieve or don't achieve your dreams and goals. A person who possesses the proper level of passion and motivation can achieve incredible things. Without motivation, you might be good at something simply because of sheer talent or developed skills. But with these same skills, coupled with a clear understanding of what is at stake when achieving success in a given area, you will be an unstoppable force.

With that in mind, I created a principle that I practice called *Understanding Your Why*. Understanding your why is critical for you to achieve results, hit goals, pass milestones, etc. You will increase your chances of actually achieving your objectives, as well as make the experience of working towards your goals that much more rewarding when you know who and what is impacted by your success.

Also, when you know who and what is impacted by your success, the game takes on a whole new level of intensity. When you know why you're working as hard (and smart) as you are, and why it matters, it helps increase your motivation and desire to win. Once you understand that your action—or inaction—impacts not only yourself, but the people you hold valuable, your performance, or the desire to perform better, will skyrocket.

I discovered this philosophy early in my career while working for a large telecommunications firm in the Midwest. I was having an "off" day at work and unfortunately, a challenging client walked into our showroom. After showing the prospect a few product selections, it became apparent that this gentleman was going to be hard to work with. Rather than understanding the importance of making the sale, I let my attitude get in the way of my professionalism. I clearly did not do an effective job of winning a new client, and he walked out. I was relieved for a moment.

Luckily for me, I had established a relationship with one of my peers, and we constantly worked with each other to ensure we were executing our "A" game at work. He watched my less-than-stellar client presentation and asked what was going on. I told him how rude the client was and how glad I was that he had walked out. My friend then told me something that totally changed the way I looked at business and success from that moment on. He asked me, "Do you think that guy is going to purchase our technology?" I answered, "Yes."

My friend then said, "Don't you think your family deserves the money that would have been earned from that sale? Why did you let him go just so someone else can close the business and take that money from you?"

This stopped me in my tracks. I had been only thinking about myself. My lack of performance was now going to negatively impact my family.

Today when I work, I give 100% of everything that I can offer. I know that providing anything less than 100% will result in negative situations that impact me, as well as my family. Do you now see the importance of being the very best that you can be in all facets of your life? You must strive to be the *very best* at what you do. It literally is a matter of survival, and a matter of you being able to achieve the level of success that you and the people you care about deserve.

Fighters are normally keen observers of what's at stake regarding a win or a loss on their record, and I've seen coaches and corner men use the primal impact of loss as a motivator when their fighter is struggling to win a fight.

I once was watching a bout on television and between rounds I overheard a corner man yelling at his fighter, "If you lose this fight, think about how this will impact your wife. Think about how this will impact your daughter. This guy is trying to take food off of your table at home." The fighter, who up until that point was losing, then knocked out his opponent. I use the term *primal impact of loss* because motivation and behavior are triggered within all of us at a conscious and subconscious level.

Based on our needs as humans, it's what we do or don't do to protect, provide for, and prosper individually and as a group or family.

MASLOW'S HIERARCHY OF NEEDS

In 1943, a psychologist by the name of Abraham Maslow proposed a theory regarding the level of needs applicable to humans, as well as the conditions that needed to be met before a person could move to the next level of need satisfaction. This theory is now known as Maslow's Hierarchy of Needs, and has been used in multiple facets of physiological application ranging from identifying motivations to explaining personal behavior. Illustration 1.2 below provides a graphical representation of Maslow's pyramid and the corresponding levels of need we humans possess.

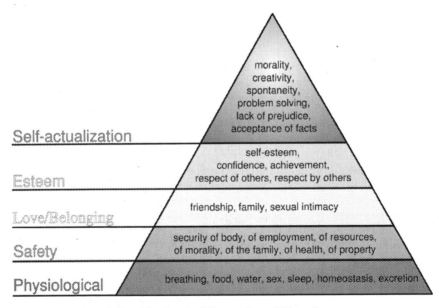

Illustration 1.2—Maslow's Hierarchy of Needs(11)

I believe the hierarchy of needs is important in understanding your "why" as it provides an excellent visual that shows how humans operate. Fundamentally, if our most basic of needs such as food, water, or safety are not properly met, we don't move to the next step of needs satisfaction. So, if you ask a starving person how they are doing relative to their confidence level or development of friendships, you're probably going to get a strange look and a response close to: "I'm starving, you fool!" Additionally, I think Maslow's theory is important because, as you will note in the grid, the sense of self is far below the need to care for others.

Most fighters will say their motivation for winning is their family, especially if they have children. Also, the family is who will be impacted from the fighter's win or loss. Many fighters know that their success is the key to their loved ones' satisfaction of primary needs such as food, shelter, and safety.

Whether your actions are of success and good intentions or of failure and negative intentions, you, and more importantly, those you hold dear, are impacted.

That sale you're about to make is going to put food on the table for your wife and children to eat. That promotion you are about to get is going to allow your kids to go to the best schools in town. That new job you just landed is going to provide health insurance for your family's protection. Everything you do has an impact and a consequence.

The principle is primal in nature, and it's extremely powerful when harnessed. This school of thought rang true with me when I first learned about Maslow's Hierarchy of Needs, because my family and loved ones come first. I'm an ultra-calm person and it takes a lot to trigger any kind of serious anger from me, so people can pretty much mess with me all day and I just laugh. Now, if someone was to mess with a close friend or a family member, that's a different story. My tolerance level is very low for that type of situation and I'm sure you are the same way.

It's human nature, and again, whether we consider it positive or negative, it is what it is, and we can use these principles to actually grow as individuals.

T.K.O. (Tips, Knowledge, and Objectives)

You can use Maslow's Hierarchy of Needs to determine your motivations and behaviors, AS WELL AS the motivations and behaviors of others. The more you understand people in general, the more you'll be able to build relationships, persuade, and perform proper conflict resolution.

SHOWTIME

Anthony "Showtime" Pettis is a great example of "understanding your why" in action. Anthony, a lightweight fighter for the UFC, fights out of Milwaukee, Wisconsin. His current fight record is 12-2-0, with his only two losses against Bart Palaszewski and Clay Guida, both equally impressive fighters. I saw Anthony fight live in 2010 in Columbus, Ohio, and his bout with Danny Castillo was incredible. Unknown to me during his fight was the fact that his family was sitting in front of the group I was with, and after he won his fight against Castillo, he came into the stands and spent time with his family. I remember looking at this guy and thinking that he's got a solid future ahead of him; and while he's a beast in the cage, it's good to see that he was grounded enough to immediately connect with his family after his bout.

Later in 2010, MTV broadcasted a show called "World of Jenks" and Anthony was featured in the episode titled "Fifty Fists." The show provided an excellent overview of Anthony's commitment to fighting, as well as his commitment to his local community and fan base. What struck me most was that Anthony allowed the camera to see personal details of his life that still drive and motivate, but unfortunately, also haunt him to this day.

Anthony's father was stabbed and murdered during a robbery, and not only was this emotionally traumatic, it also put Anthony in a position where today he needs to provide financially for his family. Anthony fights in honor and in memory of his father, and he also fights to ensure those he holds closest to him are cared and provided for.

Anthony's loss to Palaszewski put him in a position where he felt that he had to win against Castillo or there was a good chance that he would be fired. If Anthony had been let go, this likely would have negatively impacted his immediate family, and delayed or eliminated the success he would gain by becoming a champion fighter. Anthony knows why he fights. He knows why he has to train like a man possessed; he knows why he needs to win his fights, and he knows what is at stake with every win.

Not only did Anthony win against Danny Castillo, he went on a three fight win streak, and won the championship belt with the WEC before the organization merged with the UFC.

Anthony understands his "why" and he's using this powerful principle to take action and accomplish his dreams and care for the people he cares for most in life.

PUTTING THE "WHY" IN ACTION

Pursuing your dreams and achieving greatness can expose people to some very trying times. If achieving success was easy, everyone would have done it. I believe that when you put effort towards something you appreciate the rewards much more. I once heard an ancient curse that, paraphrased, states, may all of your dreams be immediately and effortlessly filled. Basically, it means that if you always get everything you want without any effort or risk, your life will be uneventful and without passion or excitement. The television show *The Twilight Zone* aired an episode called "A Nice Place to Visit" in the 1960's. This episode was about a crook who died and was sent to a place where he was given everything he wanted without any effort on his part. If he asked someone to hand over their wallet, they would do it, and the wallet would be full of cash. If he gambled, he won every time. If he entered a room full of women, he would capture their attention immediately. If he played pool, he would win every time. It was great for him at first, but after a while he grew tired of how easy things were to obtain and then he grew frustrated.

Finally, he went to the man he thought was his guardian angel and asked if he could leave, as he could no longer take the monotony of Heaven and wanted to live instead in Hell. His "guardian angel" then said, "Heaven, Mr. Valentine? Whatever gave you the idea that you were in Heaven? This is <u>the other place</u>!"

My point here is not that you have to suffer in order to achieve success, but understand that the work you have to perform, the sweat you have to drop, the rejection you have to face, the crap you have to take, is challenging, but it will make the "prize" that much sweeter when you achieve it. You just have to remember your "why." If you lose track or focus on this, it becomes so easy to just give in.

So many stories within the history of the world, including modern times, illustrate challenges, failures, and frustrations that people had to endure before they achieved their dreams. The world of MMA has hundreds of stories that illustrate this fact. The worlds of acting, writing, and music are also chock full of stories where people were near or completely at the bottom of existence, only to hit it huge because they hung on and fought so they could achieve greatness and support themselves and those they cared for the most. Personally, I've had times when the proverbial "stuff has hit the fan" and I just wanted to quit what I was doing. Right before I decided to "pull the plug" and quit, I remembered why and for whom I was fighting and I continued to fight. In almost every case it paid off and I'm glad I pushed through the crap to achieve what I was looking to complete.

What about you?

What are you fighting for in life? Who are you fighting for? What's at stake if you win or if you lose? Do you keep the things and the people for which you're fighting in your mind when you have to dig deep to achieve success or complete a goal?

If you're a student working to achieve a degree, are you willing to pull all-nighters if needed in order to study to ace an exam? What would achieving a 4.0 GPA mean to you and your current or future family and loved ones?

If you're a business owner, are you willing to work years with the potential of just scraping by financially? What would building a business that later generated millions of dollars for you in income mean to your current or future children? How about the money that you could later donate to help build your community or fund projects for organizations that you support?

If you're a sales person, are you willing to face rejection and hear the word "no" over and over again before you hear the magic word "yes" when selling your products or services? Who in your life is going to be positively impacted when you bring home that bonus check for exceeding your sales quota? What are the fun events you can plan with your family and friends to celebrate your successes?

Determining your "why" is a simple enough exercise and yet its results can be profound. Please complete the following steps to identify your primary drivers and clearly pinpoint the impact that achieving outrageous client satisfaction will have on your life.

RULES OF THE OCTAGON

Rule #2: Understand your why:

Step one: Grab a piece of paper and copy the fields listed below.

Family: How will they be impacted when you achieve additional success?

_____   _____

_____   _____

_____   _____

_____   _____

Friends: How will they be impacted when you achieve additional success?

_____   _____

_____   _____

_____   _____

_____   _____

Hobbies & Interests: How will they be impacted when you achieve additional success?

_____   _____

_____   _____

_____   _____

_____   _____

Spirituality & Community: What else can you give when you achieve additional success?

_____   _____

_____   _____

_____   _____

_____   _____

Step two: On the right side of the paper, in the "How will they be impacted when I achieve additional success," you will write down the direct benefits that the associated party will receive after you achieve the level of success you are working towards. In the family column, the impact might be things such as providing your children with access to educational programs that will help them grow. It might be your ability to finally buy the engagement ring you've wanted to purchase for your fiancée. In the friend column, it might be something like funding a trip to visit your best friend who lives in another state. In the hobbies column, the impact might be your ability to attend an MMA training seminar or an MMA live event. In the spirituality and community column, the impact might be increasing your contribution to your church or funding a project to help children in your community. The direct benefits are things that only you know about, and thus it's important that you really think about them and write them down in detail.

Step Three: Paste your "why" statement in a place where you will be constantly reminded of why you're doing what you're doing, and why you're striving to be the very best.

Remember, if you're aware of what's at stake when you achieve success, you will be unstoppable. Those who work with understanding their impact might generate success but not with the passion, focus, or effectiveness of knowing the whole reach of all your efforts. Use this technique and I promise that you'll see results as you implement the material covered in this book.

Below is an example of what your "why" statement can look like, based upon ideas and statements that I've seen in the past.

Family: How will they be impacted when
                           you achieve additional success?

Mary_____   **I can take Mary on that vacation to Rome she's always wanted**
Sami_____   **I can help Sami pay for her first year of college**
Joel_____   **I can help Joel purchase his first car**

Friends: How will they be impacted when
                           you achieve additional success?

Rick _____   **I can help cover the expenses for our annual fishing trip**
Tom _____   **I can help Tom pay some of his medical expenses**
Bill_____   **I can take Bill to see an MMA event in Vegas**

Hobbies & Interests: How will they be impacted when
                           you achieve additional success?

MMA_____   **I will be able to attend an advanced grappling course**
Drums_ _____   **I will be able to purchase a new drum kit**
Fishing_____   **I will be able to attend the annual fishing trip with the boys**
Golf_____   **I will be able to golf at least once a week**

Spirituality & Community: What else can you give when you achieve additional success?

Humane Society__   **I will be able to donate pet food and my time to the HS**
Boys Club _____   **I will be able to help pay for a basketball hoop at the center**
Church _____   **I will be able to increase my tithe from 8% to 10%**

Obviously, the people and goals you list will vary, but you can see that areas of impact can range from funding family educational needs to going on fishing trips with friends. No item is too small or too large, as long as what you write resonates with you. The more passionate you are about who and what you add to your "why" list, the more this exercise will motivate you to use it to generate results; and if you use this exercise, you will see results. You will know what is at stake if you succeed or if you fail. You will have visual representation of those you hold closest to you and what it is that you're working to achieve in life. Use it and make it work for you today.

T.K.O. (Tips, Knowledge, and Objectives)

Telling other people why and what motivates and drives you is a great way to connect with people, as well as allow other people to help you achieve your goals. I once saw a sales rep include a picture of his daughter in a PowerPoint presentation to discuss why clients should purchase his technology. The picture initially made people laugh when they saw it, but I think it also made people connect with this presenter and his presentation received incredibly positive feedback from clients.

THE SCORECARD

- *IDENTIFY, DOCUMENT, AND KEEP VISIBLE A REMINDER OF THE PEOPLE AND THE THINGS YOU'RE WORKING FOR IN YOUR LIFE*
- *REMEMBER, WHAT YOU DO IMPACTS YOUR LOVED ONES (BOTH POSITIVELY AND NEGATIVELY)*
- *GIVE 100% WHEN YOU COMMIT TO SOMETHING AND WORK TO BE THE BEST AT THESE EFFORTS*

Chapter
3

Understanding and Eliminating Fear

"You put the Devil on the other side, and I will come to fight."—Royce Gracie(12)

ANTICIPATION OF THE UNEXPECTED

I'll never forget the first time I went into the fighter's area at a mixed martial arts event. The fights were sponsored by the Legends of Fighting (LFC) organization in Indianapolis, Indiana. The event was hosted at a local bar called the "8 Second Saloon", which was a smoky, dark establishment that hosted not only LFC events, but also a good number of rock and country music shows from local and national recording artists. I entered the bar and received a wristband which designated me as a second (corner) and then I made my way into the back area of the bar which was being used as the fighter's locker rooms. I met up with my friends and then caught up with the local fighter I was there to support. The fighter is calm and laid back, as if he's there to just talk with friends rather than jump into a cage with an opponent who's hell bent on knocking him out.

I then looked around and saw that not all fighters shared the calm and cool approach to pre-fight preparations as he did that night. One of the things that I respect about many MMA fighters is the fact that they are brave enough to mention that they're nervous. I hear comments such as, "Man, I'm nervous about this fight," and, "My nerves are on the edge right now" several times throughout the evening. Whether it's admitted or not, I think all of the fighters are at least a little nervous about their upcoming bout. As any MMA fighter will tell you, anything can happen in MMA. A highly trained Muay Thai (striking) fighter can get knocked out by a highly trained wrestler simply because of a well-timed and well-placed punch. Everyone has a puncher's chance, and with that in mind, it's easy to understand why a fighter might be nervous or concerned about the outcome of their fight. Anything can happen.

I made my way into the restroom area located within the fighter's area and was immediately greeted by a pool of puke on the floor at the entrance of the bathroom. Apparently, someone's nerves had gotten the best of them. After leaving the restroom and going back into the fighter's area, the energy of the room was tangible. The experience of being in an environment like that was both nerve wracking and addicting, plus you learn an incredible amount about the human condition and how we deal with fear.

UNDERSTANDING FEAR

A wise person once said that fear stands for False Evidence Appearing Real, and if you think about it, this theory makes a lot of sense. How many things have you worried about in your life, only to later realize that the thing you were worried about never happened? Motivational leader Dale Carnegie once said, "You can conquer almost any fear if you will only make up your mind to do so. For remember, fear doesn't exist anywhere except in the mind."(13) Fear is the way the human mind prepares itself to handle a situation, but fear can also be an incredibly limiting factor that robs people of success. US President Franklin D. Roosevelt said that, "The only thing we have to fear is fear itself,"(14) and this statement has helped not only individuals, but an entire nation through hard times. A failure to understand and eliminate fears can have a huge impact on the amount of greatness that is achieved by an individual, and yet some people will allow their fears to run rampant within their lives. Some fears, such as the fear of heights or fear of flying, can easily be identified, but other fears, such as the fear of succeeding, can be deep rooted and even subconscious in nature.

Some fears, such as the fear of dying, can seem obvious and logical in nature, but fear is a complex topic and people can suffer from debilitating fear of things such as:

- Acousticophobia—The fear of noise
- Agiliophobia—The fear of pain
- Amaxophobia—The fear of driving in a car
- Achuophobia—The fear of darkness

That's just the tip of the iceberg and just a fraction of the known phobias. A much broader and equally complex type of fear that impacts millions of people (and many times they don't even know it) is the fear of success and the fear of failure. The fear of success is the deep-rooted fear that makes people concerned about what will happen to them if they actually achieve a degree of success in their lives. They worry about things such as being known for something great and then failing to live up to people's future expectations. They worry about things such as the problems of having too much money, too much fame, or too many people involved in their lives. They worry about achieving great things and then losing them because of not being able to sustain greatness. Rather than subject themselves to this level of worry and stress, they derail and self-destruct right before or immediately after achieving a degree of success.

The fear of failure makes people doubt their skills and abilities before they even take action to complete a task that might generate success for them.

They worry about looking bad in front of people, losing money or time, and failing. This fear will keep people from even attempting to achieve success, or it can extremely limit the extent of their performance or work.

Fear is natural and to a certain degree a positive thing when it is used to avoid danger or provide adrenaline to the body when needed. When discussing the topic of the fear of public speaking, news anchorman Walter Cronkite once said that, "It's natural to have butterflies. The secret is to get them to fly in formation."(15)

Imagine what our world would be like today if the early explorers did not overcome their fear that the Earth was flat and the thought that they would plummet to their death once they came to the edge.

Imagine what the United States would be like today if the early settlers were too afraid to even make the voyage in the first place. Imagine what it would be like if NASA wasn't able to find astronauts to fly to the moon because everyone was too afraid of being catapulted into orbit in a super compact vessel. Our history is full of stories and examples where bravery has overcome fear. We have accomplished feats where grit and confidence have achieved success when it would have been much easier to just run away from the situation in the first place. What would our world be like if fear dominated our lives, and what is fear holding you back from today?

Is it your dream to become an MMA fighter for one of the major fighting organizations? Is it your dream to stand in front of thousands of people and conduct a motivation seminar? Is it your dream to own your own business? Is it your dream to become the President of your company? It doesn't matter what you're striving for, each goal or dream can contain a degree of fear that you will have to overcome.

Can you imagine the fear that you might feel if you were a UFC fighter and Shane Carwin or Brock Lesnar was standing across from you? When UFC 117 aired on pay per view television on July 3, 2010, I remember being amazed at how large both of these guys were when they were in their corners ready to pounce on each other.

I'd imagine that anyone in the position of having to take on a guy the size of either one of them might be a little nervous. Fear is the element that provides fuel to the "fight or flight" instinct. When faced with a situation that causes your mind and body to think "Oh crap!" you will be provided with the emotions and energy that tell your body to run like hell or stay and dominate. Power is provided to the person who understands how to use this energy and make it into a positive thing, while eliminating the negative aspect that it might bring.

CONQUERING FEAR—GAINING CONFIDENCE

When a person is aware of their fear and works to understand and embrace it, they take a big step towards eliminating it. The first way to address and eliminate negative fear is by gaining confidence. UFC Hall of Famer Ken Shamrock once said, "It's about having confidence in yourself. I'm not afraid of that man across from me."(16) One gains confidence by knowledge and/or successful practice and experience. If you know you can do something, it's less likely that you fear it. If you've already done something successfully, it's less likely that you'll fear it the second time you approach it. Confidence in your abilities is the key.

Brazilian Jiu-Jitsu legend and UFC Hall of Famer Royce Gracie once said, that anything he decided to do in life, he would be the best at it. Obviously, this is a man who has confidence in himself and his abilities, but Royce Gracie is also a man who has invested hours upon hours mastering his craft. He knows that he would need to invest the appropriate amount of time to master whatever field he decided to enter, but he also knows that he has the required discipline that it would take to master the field. So how do you gain confidence if you're lacking it now?

The first step is gaining and maintaining belief in yourself. UFC fighter Diego "The Dream" Sanchez is known for his passion and his strong self-belief. He is famous for his level of motivation and the way he generates positive energy (Youtube "yes cartwheel") and the energy he creates is infectious and obviously effective. Diego has said, "When I step into the ring, I want to have 100 percent of my energy, I want to thrive off the energy of the fans in the crowd, and of course, my main helper is my lord and savior, Jesus Christ. I just feel that God is the one who keeps me calm and helps me not let that get to me. It also comes down to me being very confident, because if I'm not confident, then I'm gonna start to have doubts and start to think about the bad things that can happen to me in the cage—like getting knocked out or submitted or cut. If I think about those things, it's gonna be on my mind and it's gonna bring me down. I stay positive, I stay focused, and I think about what I have to do to beat my opponent."[17]

If Diego, or any other fighter for that matter, jumped into the cage and said, "I hope I can win," or "Maybe, I might win," chances are that they would get defeated simply because they lacked the true confidence that would have allowed them to seek the path of victory. Whether you're in business, going to school, or working to become the next MMA world champion, you have to have an abundance of confidence.

One of the best ways to develop confidence in something that perhaps you've never actually done is to act as if you've already completed the task or action that you're working to achieve. Act as if you've already made that sale, aced that test, or won your fight. Embrace how this makes you feel.

Change your posture to reflect the way that you would stand up after achieving success. Talk to people with the confidence that you would exhibit after achieving success. Get rid of words such as *hope*, *maybe*, and *if*. Talk and think as though you have achieved what you have set out to achieve. As the English poet John Dryden once said, "For they conquer who believe they can,"(51) and these are powerful words.

CONQUERING FEAR—GAIN EXPERIENCE

One of the most powerful ways to conquer fear is to have already successfully achieved positive results and effectively completed tasks and actions. Unfortunately, not all of us are afforded this luxury in all aspects of life, but what we can start doing is gaining as much experience in a given endeavor as soon as possible.

For example, most people who want to be a pilot do not immediately jump in an airplane and start flying around. It takes hours and hours of training to become a certified pilot, and the cost per hour for this training is relatively expensive. So, if flying is a passion for you and yet you cannot attend the formal training just yet, does this mean you cannot get any exposure to flying? Of course it doesn't. If you own a computer, you can invest in a comprehensive flight software program.

You can go to your local library and check out books, CD's, DVD's, and training manuals on the subject of flying. You can even go to local flight training institutes and talk with instructors about your goals and desires. They might be able to provide you with material that will help you along, or maybe you will even start to build relationships that might gain you access to things such as being able to fly as a guest during a flight session. The point here is that if you're passionate about achieving success, dive in as quickly as possible and start gaining experience in whatever element of the endeavor you're looking to master. What you'll find is that the micro-experience you gain becomes macro-experience over time. Like the old saying goes, "How do you eat an elephant?" The answer is "One bite at a time."

In the world of MMA, most fighters do not jump into the cage on day one without any experience of fighting mixed martial arts. It is said that UFC fighter Clay Guida's first MMA fight happened when he went to go see a local MMA bout, but then jumped into the cage to actually fight that night. Clay also got his butt kicked while doing it, but luckily, the bout motivated Clay to obtain formal training and today he is one of the most dynamic fighters in the cage.

Start gaining as much experience with the things you are looking to accomplish. The more experience you gain, the more comfortable you will feel with the process, as well as your abilities. The more comfortable you feel, the less nervous and fearful you will be. When your mind is calm, it allows you to focus, to concentrate, to block out unnecessary distractions, and this calmness will generate great results for you.

CONQUERING FEAR—ANALYZE YOUR FEAR

Another way to conquer your fear is to analyze exactly why you're afraid of something in the first place. I once heard a story about a child in a small village who was told to never go into a nearby cave. When the child asked his mother why he couldn't go into the cave, she told him that it was just the rule of the village and it was rumored that a mountain lion lived in the cave. When the boy asked his father about the cave, he was told that a large boar lived in the cave and that it was a village rule to not venture there. Now the boy was curious because his mom said it was a lion and his dad said it was a boar that lived in the caves, so he wondered which one was right. The boy then went to his grandmother and asked her why he couldn't go into the caves. She smiled and told him to ask his grandfather this question. When the boy asked his grandfather why no one in the village could go into the caves, the old man laughed and told the boy that when his parents were children about his age, the village men would use the caves to make and store their booze for village parties.

In an effort to keep the kids out, the fathers would tell the kids about killer bears, boars, lions, and monsters, to keep them from venturing into the caves. Once the village women found out about the booze, the men stopped using the caves for their drunken activities.

Apparently, they didn't want the kids to know about the fibs they had been told, because more than likely they wouldn't believe anything they were told in future, so everyone forgot about the cave stories . . . except the kids who were now parents.

So a little white lie that was created to keep kids out of a booze stash turned into fear that was created and then passed down to another generation of kids. The thing I like about this story is that the kid questioned what was going on in the caves and didn't just choose to believe the stories, thus allowing unwarranted fear in his life.

Fear, of things both perceived and real, can grip people in some very strange and incredible ways. It can make you believe things that are farfetched and almost too crazy to believe. I remember when I was about eleven years old, my younger stepbrother told me about the day he was attacked by witches and goblins in his room. I laughed at his story and probably called him stupid or something like that. The odd thing was that when he was around ten years old, I brought up that same story, and he once again told me the event actually happened to him. It wasn't until a couple years later that he finally admitted he must have been dreaming and there was no way he was actually attacked by witches and goblins.

The point here is that this memory and re-validation of the memory was something that stuck with him from the ages of five to eleven or twelve. Something as goofy as little miniature witches lodged their way into his consciousness and sub-consciousness and took up residence for several years.

Do you have things in your life that you currently fear? If so, have you ever stopped and really thought about why you possess this fear in the first place? Was it something that happened to you in your childhood? Are they fears that were imposed on you from external sources such as family, friends, society, or community? If you can identify the root cause or source of your fear, how valid is it now that you really think about it? Some fears are deep rooted and their root cause is not easy to identify. For example, I have a mild case of claustrophobia, and I have no idea why. One time when I was in the Navy, I was on a Mediterranean cruise aboard the aircraft carrier USS John F. Kennedy. On a carrier, your bed space is literally an eight-foot-long cube that serves as a sleeping space and storage area. Also, the bunks are stacked three beds high, so there's a bunk on the ground, one in the middle, and one on top. During my first cruise I was the guy in the middle bunk and I quickly ran into an interesting discovery of my claustrophobia. The bunks have dark curtains that cover the sleeping space, so when you go to sleep and they turn out the lights, it gets pretty dark in the beds. So, one night I went to bed and I dreamed that the guys in my shop put me in a small box and sat on the top of it so I couldn't get out.

I started yelling in the box and then slammed my fists on top of the box as hard as I could. All of a sudden, the curtains in my bunk slammed open and the guy who was sleeping on the top bunk was yelling, "Dude, what is your problem?"

I was actually wide awake screaming and slamming on the top of my bunk ceiling and scared the crap out of the guy in the top bed.

My heart was racing and I was sweating from the fear. From that point on, I slept with the curtains cracked a bit and I realized that tight spaces kind of get to me at times. Why was I concerned with tight spaces? To my memory, I never experienced a situation as a child that would trigger this fear. I never experienced an event where I saw someone get hurt or die due to confinement, so when I ran into the fear myself, it perplexed me. With that said, because I recognized the fear, I know how to work with it today. If I'm in a tight space I know to just breathe and relax. By identifying the things that can limit you, you are able to reduce their impact, as well as learn how to work past them. Take the time to identify your fears and then really try to understand why you have them, and equally important, what you can do to reduce or remove their impact on you in the future.

T.K.O. (Tips, Knowledge, and Objectives)

Avoid negative sources of energy and information. Have you ever noticed how the media predominately reviews and highlights bad news and negative things going on in the world? The reason for that is people are instinctively drawn to the negative because we want to know what can harm us, as well as what to avoid. If you stay aware of negative outlets of data and influence, the number of things that cause you concern and fear will be reduced.

CONQUERING FEAR—
REALITY VERSUS PERCEPTION

There's an old saying that states *perception equals reality*. In other words, what people perceive to be true is true to them no matter if it's real or not. In 1999, Daniel Simons and Christopher Chabris, two college professors and doctors in the field of psychology, conducted a humorous but amazing project called "the invisible gorilla" experiment(18). If you've not seen this experiment before, stop reading, and go to Youtube.com, and search for "selective attention test". When you follow the instruction of the video in detail, you might be surprised at the results. Go check it out now, and then come back to this book.

About half the people who watch this video will not see the gorilla show up during the experiment. When I first watched the video it shocked me because I would have bet a hundred dollars that there wasn't a gorilla in the video, and yet there is. This experiment is incredibly powerful because it illustrates the power of focus, attention, and perception. If you see or don't see something, it can define how you make decisions, act, and register your overall effectiveness in business, relationships, and life in general.

What we focus on in life creates the perception of our reality. We fear the things we perceive as things to fear, regardless if the fear is valid or logical.

When you find yourself concerned or in fear of something, always ask these questions and follow this process:

1. Ask yourself, "What is it that I'm concerned about?"
2. Identify, "What about this thing do I know to be 100% true?"

3. Identify what about this thing is just speculation or not 100% known.

4. After identifying the known and unknown aspects of your fear, if you find that most elements of your fear are not known to be 100% confirmed, your fear is perceived and not validated.

5. Acknowledge that your concern is perception and gain power over it.

Let me give you an example of my philosophy. When I was a child around the age of nine, I was very afraid of the movie *The Exorcist*. It scared me even more once I heard it was based on a true story. The only problem with this condition was the fact that I never even saw the movie, but was afraid of it. I had heard how scary it was from my parents. I then heard stories about how the movie caused people to have heart attacks in the theatre, and I knew for sure that if the devil had possessed a little girl, there was always the chance that my rear was next. Years later, I actually saw the movie and it was scary, so my perceived fear was now validated.

Then I started to hear about other new movies that were even scarier than *The Exorcist*. At first this freaked me out because the movie was super scary and I could not imagine a movie capable of frightening me even more.

So when I watched these new movies, knowing I was going to get the living crap scared out of me, something funny happened. None of them frightened me. My fear of the other movies was based on the false perception that they would compare to *The Exorcist*, and they didn't. Perceived fear can expand itself into other areas of your life, thus causing greater fear, as well as falsely validating your original concerns. Always analyze your fears to ensure that what you're concerned about is actually real and known, and not just a perception.

CONQUERING FEAR—GAIN FEEDBACK

An excellent way to reduce erroneous internal perception is to ask for external feedback. In other words, if after a performance or completing something, you find yourself thinking things such as, "I think that might have sucked," or "I don't think that was good; I wonder what others thought," obtain the answers by asking those who saw your performance and are involved in the same task or situation in which you are. If you tell someone that you're looking to improve yourself and would appreciate their honest and detailed feedback, chances are that they will give it to you.

Remember, loved ones and people reluctant to hurt your feelings might sugar-coat some of your areas of improvement, so seek out advice from people you know will be upfront and honest, but will also provide feedback in a non-brutal way.

In other words, if your performance was lacking, just as you don't want your wife or parents telling you that you did wonderful (when you didn't), you also don't want a jerk friend to say something like, "God, you sucked so bad I thought your name was vacuum!" Feedback needs to be honest and delivered in a positive way. Remember, when you ask someone for their input, shut up and listen to what they have to say.

It's not always easy to listen to criticism, especially when you're talking about your dream or something you're fighting for, but you'll never get better until you listen and replay back to the person what you think you just heard them say to you. Listening is more important than talking, which is why God gave you two ears and just one mouth. When you receive feedback from someone, write down what they have to say and monitor your progress with these items in the future. If someone tells you that during your speech you said "ummmm" and "uhhhh" several times and it became distracting, write this down and focus on doing your speeches and being cognizant of not making these noises. If you receive feedback and do nothing with it, you're wasting your time, as well as the person who's trying to help you improve with their feedback.

Feedback can be received before, during, and after your performance or work has been completed. If you ever watch MMA fighters in training, their coaches and fellow fighters in training provide constant feedback to help a fighter prepare for a bout.

Between rounds of an MMA fight, a fighter will have corner-men and coaches actually come into the cage and provide feedback on the previous round, as well as guidance on what they need to do differently, or more of, in the upcoming round. Afterwards, fighters will watch footage of the fight to see what they did wrong and what they need to focus on to improve in the future. Gaining feedback is critical because remember this, you are your own worst enemy and you will almost always be more brutal on yourself than will anyone around you. If you always listen only to the internal critic called your mind, you might only be getting half of the story. Listen to others and to people you've specifically asked to review your performance and provide you with guidance.

T.K.O. (Tips, Knowledge, and Objectives)

Course correct your path towards success by using the feedback you obtain from trusted advisors. When a plane flies from one destination to another, it doesn't do so by following a completely straight path. The plane moves off course multiple times during a trip and the pilot corrects the course until the destination is reached. Your life will be the same. You might move off course from time to time, but use feedback and guidance to get back on track and achieve results.

CONQUERING FEAR—POSITIVE VISUALIZATION

The great motivational leader and author Napoleon Hill once said, "Whatever your mind can conceive and believe it can achieve."(19) This statement is powerful in so many ways, because it so eloquently illustrates the power of the mind. Your mind, and how you train it, is the key to your success in whatever endeavor you do in life. Your mind is so powerful that it will provide you with guidance to learn consciously, subconsciously, with your eyes open, and even with your eyes completely closed. Whether you're actually doing a task or just walking through the process in your mind, your brain will process the experience and provide outcomes and solutions.

When you visualize yourself completing a task, your brain will walk through the experience and actually allow you to apply a form of training that will help you when you perform the task in real life. I once watched a television show about the Blue Angels, the U.S. Navy's elite flying team. During the show, the stunt team allowed the cameras to record a remarkable part of their event training. Before the pilots board their multi-million dollar aircrafts and perform some of the most amazing air maneuvers you can imagine, they actually imagine the performance in detail. The pilots will gather around a table, close their eyes, and get in the position that their bodies take when they are flying.

With his arms extended in front of him, the lead pilot grabs his imaginary joystick and leads the team through a step-by-step process of the event, from wheels up to landing finale.

When you walk through a process in your mind, you allow yourself to start processing how you will manage certain situations and you course correct as needed. Visualization can be applied to almost anything you can think of. If you have a big speech that you need to make, visualize yourself completing the task from the point that you step up to the podium, to the time when you're finished answering questions and receiving applause. If you're about to go on a big job interview, visualize yourself entering the office, shaking your interviewer's hand, answering detailed and complex questions about your qualifications, closing the deal on why they should hire you, and then leaving the interview with a job offer. As children, we are naturally good with the process of visualization. Do you remember pretending to be an astronaut on a voyage to the moon? Remember playing shop, doctor, and house? Humans are blessed with this thing called imagination and imagination is not only helpful to create fantasies in our minds, but it also helps you conduct detailed role-play and effectively visualize how you will manage and handle situations. The following are tips and techniques on how to properly use visualization for greater success.

1. Find a place where you will be undisturbed for 10-15 minutes.
2. Sit in a comfortable position, close your eyes, and begin taking deep breaths in from your nose and exhaling out from your mouth.
3. Relax and continue this breathing pattern for two to three minutes.
4. Now, with your eyes closed, imagine yourself at the earliest stages of the process or action you want to complete.

5. From this point, imagine as much detail as possible. Create the experience to be as real in your mind as possible.

6. See yourself completing the next step in the process. Imagine multiple situations that might develop within the step. Perhaps it's a difficult question that you might have to answer, an objection that a client throws at you, or maybe a technique that you applied in a different way than you normally do.

7. See yourself effectively handling any situation that comes your way. Provide yourself with experience on how to handle multiple outcomes that might develop.

8. Close the visualization with success. Always see yourself achieving the goal or outcome you desire.

9. Repeat often before the actual process or action takes place.

People sense confidence and are drawn towards people they feel are confident and who get the job done. Even if you've never actually done something before, if you've provided your mind with enough time to work through possible scenarios, you will look a lot more prepared and experienced compared to just waiting until the day of an event and hoping like hell that you're prepared for it. Prepare for it mentally and come equipped for success physically and mentally.

CONQUERING FEAR—
HARNESS THE POWER OF "PMI"
(POSITIVE MENTAL ATTITUDE)

Negative energy and negative attitudes are a cancer that kills dreams and wrecks lives. Unfortunately, negative energy, just like quicksand, will suck you in and make release almost impossible. Negative energy and information surround us constantly. If you read the newspaper or read the news on the Internet, chances are that you will be bombarded with negative stories. Even at this moment as I open a press update on the Internet, I see articles that address subjects such as: "Five children killed after fire engulfs Florida home, "Money is big issue in stress survey," as well as a plethora of political and social fodder to wade through if one desires. People are drawn to negative press, whether or not we want to accept this fact. The reason why people are more drawn to bad news over good news is due to a psychological protection factor. In other words, you want to know about the good things going on amongst your friends, family, community, and the world, but it's also human nature to be aware of things that might potentially bring you harm. Fear gains priority over most cognitive thinking.

Imagine that you're walking down a street on your way to a store to pick up groceries. While on your way to the store, you mentally make a list of the items you want to purchase. You have not eaten all day and your stomach is making all kinds of sounds from being empty. It starts to make more noise as you think about the steaks and potatoes that you're going to purchase and eat for dinner that night, but all you can think about at the moment is your severe hunger.

Then all of a sudden, you see a large dog come barreling out of a house and running in your direction. The dog is barking loudly and baring his sharp teeth as he gets closer to you. Guess what? You're no longer worried about your hunger pains.

A new, more powerful emotion and set of concerns have entered your mind and hunger has quickly been demoted towards the bottom of your immediate worries.

Fear gains priority because as humans we try to avoid situations that could cause us death or severe harm, and this is why people want to know about what to avoid in the first place. This is why negative news gains higher ratings than good news, and this is why many people are surrounded by a constant bombardment of negative energy.

As a person seeking the path of success, you must discipline yourself to avoid negativity. The reduction of negativity in your life will be in direct proportion to your reduction and/or elimination of fear. The more stress, problems, and worries that you expose yourself to, the greater you will fear things that are outside of your control, and more than likely not even impacting your life in the first place. The godfather of positive thinking and author of *The Power of Positive Thinking*, Norman Vincent Peale, wrote that we should "formulate and stamp indelibly on your mind a mental picture of yourself as succeeding. Hold this picture tenaciously. Never permit it to fade. Your mind will seek to develop the picture . . . Do not build up obstacles in your imagination."[20]

Exposing yourself to superfluous and irrelevant negativity is how you build up the obstacles in your imagination that Mr. Peale warns us about in his writing.

Making problems where there are no problems is how people develop stress and unnecessary anxiety in their lives. Starting today, ensure that you are avoiding negativity and exposing yourself to positive outlets of information. Refuse to be drawn into the vortex of negativity and maintain a positive outlook on life. The more positive you are in life, the less you will fear. Plus, your positivity will become infectious and you'll help other people avoid being negative. A residual effect is that you'll soon become known as the "positive one" and people will like being around you. Make a change in what you expose yourself to on a daily basis and how you allow negativity to affect you, and you'll begin to see remarkable changes in your life.

CONQUERING FEAR—EMBRACE IT

Eleanor Roosevelt said, "You gain strength, courage, and confidence by each experience in which you really stop to look fear in the face. You are able to say to yourself 'I have lived through this horror. I can take the next thing that comes along.' You must do the thing you think you cannot do."(21) Whether its cage fighting or completing a thesis for a doctorate degree, we all have mountains to climb and monsters to slay as they relate to completing tasks in our lives. If you desire success and want to generate results in your life (which is obviously the case since you're reading this book) there are going to be times when you have to grab the proverbial bull by the horns and set aside your fear. When you do this, you'll find out that something incredible will happen . . . you'll stop fearing the thing that initially caused you fear and you'll be able to take on even larger and potentially scarier tasks in your life. Let me give you an example.

During my time in the United States Navy, I worked as an Aviation Ordnanceman and loaded missiles on the F-14 Tomcat aircraft. As I mentioned previously, I completed two Mediterranean cruises aboard the U.S.S. John F. Kennedy; working aboard an aircraft carrier has been classified as one of the most dangerous jobs in the world. During my first cruise, as rookies working the flight deck, we were provided with initial guidance as far as how to move around on the flight deck, as well as some basic safety trips. The Petty Officer that ran my shop was fairly straightforward as far as his warnings about the flight deck.

He told us, "You do everything I tell you or I will guarantee you that you'll either be sucked up in a jet's engine or blown over the side of the ship," and this scared the crap out me. I knew that I had to get used to working on the flight deck and yet I was nervous as hell. The day came when we were finally allowed to step foot on the flight deck and four of us rookies were led around the deck by hanging on to the belt loop of the guy in front of us.

We basically looked like little baby ducks being led around by the daddy duck, our shop manager, the guy ready to bite the head off the first one of us that did something we weren't supposed to do. I'll never forget that first day on the flight deck. All of the fighter jets were closer to each other than I had expected. As the jets turned on the deck, you would feel this instant and intense blast of searing heat hit your face. The crews preparing the jets kept up a frantic pace, and with all the action and intensity of the moment, I started to panic. I remember thinking to myself, "What have I gotten myself into?" but I kept following my shop manager and I did everything he told me to do.

I survived the first day and felt like I accomplished something. We weren't allowed to go on the flight deck without supervision for the first few weeks, but then something amazing started to happen. Not only did I not fear the deck, I actually started to get really good working it. I never lost respect for the deck, but I didn't fear it. I remember two separate events on the deck that proved to me that I was able to overcome and conquer things that I thought I couldn't accomplish. The first event happened during my second cruise and I was working as member of the missile arming team in my squadron.

Not only was I loading missiles on jets, I was now activating them before the aircraft was catapulted from the carrier. One time one of my jets was positioned in the very back of the carrier and we needed to activate some of the low-end explosives and anti-radar devices before the aircraft was moved to the launch area. The rear of the jet was hanging over the side of the aircraft carrier and I needed to pull a small steel pin to deactivate the safety on the device. I made my way to the back of the plane and I noticed that I had to reach out really far to pull the safety pin. I stretched and stretched but could not reach the pin. I then looked down and saw that if I positioned my foot on the top of the safety net cage, a device used to catch people who slipped off the deck, I could maneuver myself in position to pull the pin.

So here I was, standing behind a jet that had two massive engines firing on both sides of me, hanging past a safety net, the one thing that was there to save me if I did fall, and as I pulled the pin I just happened to look down and saw that there was only one leg and one metal bar between myself and a three-story drop into the ocean. While the experience was scary, I knew at the moment there wasn't much on the deck that really scared me anymore and I was ready for more. The opportunity came in the form of being promoted to run the night-shift for my shop and become part of the crew that activated and deactivated live missiles . . . at night in the pitch dark. The second event that showed that I could overcome fear occurred during one of my missile arming sessions.

I had been supervisor of the night shift for a couple of weeks and other than working in the dark and working a twelve hour shift in the middle of the night, I was getting used to the job. One night the weather turned back on us and it started to rain really hard on the deck. Now it was pitch black and my goggles started to fog up and raindrops impaired by vision even further. I was about to arm one of our jets and I just remember this huge jet coming up to the launch site and I could barely see anything. The launch officer gave the command to arm the jet and I ran up to the aircraft and pulled the pin to arm the M61A1 cannon. I then made my way under the belly of the aircraft and armed the set of Sparrow missiles loaded underneath the plane. I couldn't see anything and I was struggling to pull the pins to activate the missiles. My vision was gone, I had this monster of a plane on top of me, and now I was struggling to activate part of a jet that was partially armed with other missiles and a powerful gun system.

The odd thing was that I wasn't nervous or scared. I embraced the challenge and I stayed calm. The safety pins gave and I made my way from the jet and took my safety position as the aircraft was shot off the deck at a speed of approximately zero to one-hundred-sixty miles an hour in two seconds.

I remember thinking that if I had experienced that situation early in my deck days I would have frozen up and who knows what the hell would have happened. I didn't freeze and I embraced the fear and the stress of the moment.

Have you ever feared something but you forced yourself to complete it even though you were crazy scared? Maybe it was riding a rollercoaster, or asking someone out on a date.

Maybe it was standing up for yourself during an altercation or trying out for the wrestling team at your high school? Do you remember the fear you felt, and how good you felt about yourself after you completed the task? People who skydive, rock climb, scuba dive, and fight for a hobby or a living understand the feeling of conquering and growing past fear. The more you embrace that which you fear, the more you develop as a human and expand the level and scope of what you can accomplish during your lifetime. If you allow fear to overcome your first step, you'll never come close to stepping across the finish line. Get to the point in your life where you welcome the fear and actually feel energized about taking on the task. There is something in the pit of your stomach that feels really good when you stare at something that scares you and you say the words "Bring it on."

Nothing feels worse than knowing you walked away from something and couldn't work up the nerve to complete it or even start it due to fear. Embrace the fear, embrace the challenge, and watch your human potential soar to incredible heights.

CONQUERING FEAR—BREATHE

If you've ever cornered a fight or listened to corner-men during MMA fights, you'll hear a common instruction provided to fighters between rounds . . . breathe! Breathing provides oxygen to the brain and it also relaxes and calms people.

Getting a fighter to take deep breaths and relax their body allows the fighter to refocus and restore energy for the next round. Plus, a calm fighter will also listen to instructions more effectively.

I once gave a stress reduction talk to a group of people and I performed a little experiment on them. I asked five of the people from the audience to come up to the front of the room and have a seat. Once they sat down, I provided all of them with a bucket full of ice. At that point, I asked each of them to put their right hand into the bucket and to keep it submerged within the bucket for the next two minutes. About a minute into the process, some of the people were starting to pull their hand out of the bucket because it became too cold for them. A couple of members of the group were able to make the full two minutes, but I could tell that it was painful for them. I then asked all of them to take their hands out of the bucket and dry them off.

After their hands were dry, I turned down the lights in the room, put on some soft music, and asked the group to begin a special breathing process by taking deep breaths in through their noses and deep exhales from their mouths. We did this process for the next minute, and then I asked them to return their right hand back into the bucket of ice. This time, the results were different. No one took their hand out of the bucket and everyone made it the full two minutes. When I asked them to remove their hand from the bucket, people even mentioned that it seemed like less than two minutes. The process of effective breathing and a calm surrounding allowed the group to maintain a procedure that was previously very uncomfortable.

Pregnant women are taught a special breathing process called patterned breathing and this procedure allows many women to either deliver without an epidural to relieve pain, or greatly minimizes the amount of pain experienced while giving birth. Breathing is powerful and yet many people do not realize how it impacts them during a fearful or stressful situation. The next time you see someone who becomes angry or afraid, watch how their breathing changes. Erratic breathing can lead to loss of strength, focus, and even consciousness.

Going forward, when you find yourself in a stressful or fearful situation, be conscience of your breathing. Take deep breaths in from your nose and exhale from your mouth. Pace your breathing and remain calm. You'll quickly find that you'll be more in control of the situation and allow yourself to focus on addressing the matter at hand rather than on trying to figure out why you feel like you're ready to pass out.

Use this calm breathing process before, during, and after, a potentially stressful situation such as a presentation, a sale, or a test. If you provide your body and brain with the resources it needs, as well as allow your body to maintain control during any situation, you will reduce the impact that stress and fear can have on your body, as well as greatly increase your overall effectiveness in any given situation. Breathing is a natural body function, so use it and begin taking control of how you and your body respond to situations that cripple others.

RULES OF THE OCTAGON

Rule #3: Identify, understand, and eliminate your fears

Fear is a protection device that helps to keep us from harm and from making bad decisions, but it can also be the killer of dreams and the limiter of life. In order to overcome the unnecessary fears that hamper your success, utilize the following exercise to identify, analyze, validate, and eliminate the things that have held you back thus far in your life.

Step One—Fear Identification: Think about the things you want to accomplish in life and then write down any fears that you might have associated with tasks you'll have to take to complete these objectives. For example, maybe it is your dream to skydive, but you currently have a fear of heights.

1:_____

2:_____

3:_____

Step Two—Fear Analysis: After you have identified the things that cause or have the potential of causing you fear, write down the root cause, or why you feel this situation or condition impacts you in a negative way. For example, using our skydiving scenario above, if you have a current fear of heights, ask yourself why this causes you concern. If you are able to identify specific events or conditions that might cause the fear, write these down. Perhaps our future skydiver experienced a situation when he was a kid where he fell out of a tree house and broke his arm, and from that point he was unable to manage the thought of being in high places. If you are not able to validate your fear, right down "unknown" next to it.

FEAR	ROOT CAUSE

FEAR	ROOT CAUSE

FEAR	ROOT CAUSE

Step Three—Fear Validation: Now that you have identified and analyzed the things that might be limiting your ability to achieve success or accomplish objectives, review your root cause for validity. This part of the process is critical because it essentially requires that you look at the reason(s) behind your fears, and then reduce their validity and the stranglehold that they have on you. For example, using our skydiver one more time, if he was to apply thought to the root cause behind his fear of heights, he will start to see that elements of the fear are not valid. After he broke down the validity of the fear, he would see that his experience as a child falling from a tree and breaking his arm was an experience loaded with conditions and circumstances that were irrelevant to heights and his desire to skydive. After thinking about the root cause and validating the experience, he was able to dissect the event and he realized that he loved climbing trees before the experience. The view that he had from the top of the tree in his backyard was incredible. He climbed the tree every day and would just sit there and look around his neighborhood in awe. He realized that he fell out of the tree because a wooden step that he nailed to the tree came loose and caused him to lose his grip and fall. He remembered that his father warned him to use only good wood, five-inch steel nails, and to reinforce the wooden steps with supportive rope bands. He didn't do any of this and decided to just use his regular nails and the wood that he pulled off his old club house. The wood was weak and cracked further as he nailed it to the tree. His decision to avoid applying extra conditions of safety caused his fall. He loved being up high and just made a bad safety decision.

He really wasn't afraid of heights, just the consequences that could happen from falling. Following safety procedures and perhaps adding additional safety measures would have prevented him from harm in the past, and if he followed them in the future, he would avoid harm. By looking at the validity of his root cause he was able to identify an **"if"** statement.

An **"if"** statement is like a chink in the armor, a single hole in a dam that then breaks open. All you need to do is identify an **"if"** statement and then your brain begins to work on perimeters that will allow you to begin overcoming your fears. "I will get over my fear of water **if** I take swimming lessons." "I will get over my fear of public speaking **if** I join a Toast Masters club." These are examples of **"if"** statements that people might say when overcoming the fear of water or the fear of public speaking. Fear is only locked if you cannot identify a situation or condition that can be done to potentially reduce its impact.

Review your root causes and do two things. First, determine how valid they are in reality. Does this thing you fear even make sense or have a degree of logic behind it? If not, start telling yourself this because your brain will listen. Remember, your perception is reality and perception comes from what your brain is telling you. If you review your root causes and find validity in your fear (i.e. something happened when you last tried the experience, etc.) think about "if" statements you can use to overcome the fear. All you need is to identify the chink in the armor, even if it's a small one.

Write down as many "if" statements you can against the root cause. Start building your case to overcome the challenge.

ROOT CAUSE   **IF STATEMENT**

ROOT CAUSE   **IF STATEMENT**

ROOT CAUSE   **IF STATEMENT**

If your fears or psychological conditions are substantially impacting your most basic of life experiences and living conditions, I would recommend seeking the guidance of a psychiatrist for resolution. Your ability to overcome limiting fears, as well as effectively utilize your mind for powerful and positive programming, will put you in a position where you will be unstoppable when it comes to achieving your goals and living a fulfilling life. Once you've completed the steps outlined thus far, you will be ready for the final step of fear elimination.

Step Four—Fear Elimination: Now that you've identified your fears, analyzed and determined their root cause, applied logic/reason against the root causes to identify "if" statements, you're ready for the final set: fear elimination. The way you eliminate your fear is to use the power you have now gained over it by following the steps we've previously completed, and then you do the task you need to complete. Nike said it best, "Just do it." It may be painful; you might be close to pissing your pants, but you have to do it. If not, you'll never forgive yourself and one day, you will look back in regret. What you're doing may not even feel natural but some things in life worth pursuing don't fee, natural when you're trying to achieve them. UFC fighter Miguel Torres said, "It is not easy to get up every day and get punched in the face or work out until your muscles are screaming in agony. Everything a fighter does goes against the natural instincts of a normal human being."(22) Challenge yourself to say "bring it on" and embrace the thing you fear. The only way you will truly get over being concerned or afraid of something is to actually do it, and do it often.

It is human nature to be nervous and be cautious of some things, but it is human potential that allows us to grow past our fears and become the champions we were all meant to be. Once you've completed the action of doing the thing you fear, document it. Celebrate it. Let yourself know that you did it and it did not kill you. The saying that "What does not kill me only makes me stronger." is so true in so many different ways.

Make your list of accomplishments and watch yourself grow to incredible heights of achievement.

What I accomplished   **Date:**

1:_____ _____

2:_____ _____

3:_____ _____

THE SCORECARD

- UNDERSTAND THAT FEAR IS NATURAL AND USED AS A MECHANISM TO PROTECT US. FEAR IS ONLY BAD WHEN IT BECOMES LIMITING AND CRIPPLING IN NATURE
- BE CONFIDENT IN YOUR CAPABILITIES AND WATCH YOUR FEARS VANISH
- VISUALIZE A POSITIVE OUTCOME FOR SUCCESS
- HARNESS THE POWER OF POSSESSING A POSITIVE MENTAL ATTITUDE
- EMBRACE THE THINGS THAT CAUSE YOU FEAR. DON'T ALLOW THEM TO BREAK YOU, YOU BREAK THEM
- BREATHE!
- IDENTIFY, ANALYZE, VALIDATE, AND ELIMINATE YOUR FEARS

Chapter 4

Never Quit!

"To be honest, I don't understand that word . . . quit. If I ever go down, I'm going down in flames doing what I love." Jorge Gurgel, Strikeforce Fighter (23)

EXAMPLES OF TENACITY

Never quit! One piece of advice that is applicable to all areas of success, and one that is clearly a best practice recommendation to someone looking to generate results in their given area of focus or life objective. The world of MMA is literally an encyclopedia of "never quit" examples and situations.

UFC 111, Georges St. Pierre versus Dan Hardy. Dan Hardy, a brash but extremely talented fighter from Nottingham, England, trash talked his eventual bout with Canada's Georges St. Pierre months before the fight took place. Most fighters talk about how they are going to beat an opponent before a bout, but Hardy's verbal intimidation efforts are world famous, and for UFC 111, he took his trash talk to a new level. When the main event for UFC 111 started, Hardy had an opportunity to put his words to action and he did just that. Georges St. Pierre beat Hardy confidently every round during that fight, but during the first round of the bout, Hardy was caught in an arm bar that was almost too hard to watch because it looked like his arm was about to snap and yet Hardy didn't tap. He didn't quit.

Later in the fourth round, Hardy was caught in a tight kimura hold and even with his arm wrenched backwards in a position where it looked like his arm would snap from his shoulder, he still didn't tap. While Hardy lost the fight to Georges St. Pierre, he gained a lot of fans because the fighter clearly showed that he has the heart of a lion and would not easily stop when many others would have tapped out.

WEC 48, Leonard Garcia versus Chan Sung Jung. Garcia, or "Badboy" as he's known, fought Jung, whose nickname is the "Korean Zombie." At the beginning of the fight, the announcer, Joe Rogan, was laughing at Jung's fight nickname, but the reason why Jung is known as the "Korean Zombie" became immediately evident. For three full rounds, both Garcia and Jung traded punches at the pace and energy level that had both the crowd and the announcers shocked and enthralled. The majority of MMA fights are intense and full of highlight moments, but attacks in most fights are paced and timed as to prevent a fighter from "gassing out" or losing energy and air due to extreme cardiovascular activity. The WEC 48 event with Garcia and Jung was non-stop and any attempt to pace the fight was thrown out the window after the bell rang in the first round. With fists and kicks flying, neither fighter would quit their attack. When one fighter would strike the other would strike back. The intensity did not stop until the final bell rang at the end of round three and Garcia was awarded the decision victory. Even though Jung did not win that fight, his reputation of non-stop intensity and a never-quit heart was established that night in the minds of many MMA fans across the globe.

WEC 41,Urijah Faber versus Mike Brown. The Brown versus Faber fight at WEC 41 was actually the second time these two fighters had done battle in the cage and Mike Brown had previously beat Faber at WEC 36. Both Urijah Faber and Mike Brown are dynamic fighters, but Faber is world famous for his martial art skills, aggressive attacks, and lightning speed in the cage. Faber's speed was actually his downfall when he first fought Brown in WEC 36. Faber bounced off the cage during WEC 36 and unfortunately ran right into a punch that Brown had timed perfectly. WEC 41 was going to be the event where Faber would regain his belt from Brown and do it in dynamic fashion. Unfortunately for Faber, during the first round, he ended up breaking not one, but both hands, as he blasted at Brown. A lesser man would have stopped fighting after breaking a hand during a fight, and even rarer would be the fighter who continued to strategize on how to win a fight with two hands broken, but this is just what Faber did. Rather than use his hands, Faber started striking Brown with his elbows, as well as escalating the number of kicks in hopes of getting the chance to potentially knock Brown out during the fight.

Brown was victorious at the end of the bout, but Faber once again showed why he is known as the "California Kid" by displaying his never quit attitude. And these are just the tip of the iceberg when it comes to "never quit" examples in mixed martial arts.

PAIN IS TEMPORARY

World champion cyclist Lance Armstrong once said, "Pain is temporary. It may last a minute, or an hour, or a day, or a year, but eventually it will subside and something else will take its place. If I quit, however, it lasts forever."(24) The great inventor Thomas Edison failed at the attempt to create the light bulb over 9,000 times. It took him approximately 10,000 attempts before he succeeded. When asked by a reporter if he felt like a failure because of the unsuccessful 9,000 attempts, Edison replied, "Young man, why would I feel like a failure? And why would I ever give up? I now know definitively over 9,000 ways that an electric light bulb will not work. Success is almost in my grasp." It's staggering to think that he failed to get his light bulb to work 10,000 times and yet continued the process. Imagine if he would have stopped at 9,999 and just said to just forget about it? Imagine the progress to our society that would have been lost? Imagine the convenience that we enjoy today that wouldn't have been created, for who knows how long? When your heart and your soul is committed to achieving a goal or making progress in life, you must never quit. The majority of reasons why people quit in the first place include:

1. They don't really believe they can accomplish the goal.
2. They let other people talk them out of their dream.
3. They let setbacks create fear, uncertainty, and doubt.
4. They don't feel like they truly deserve to be successful.
5. The work to achieve success is harder than they thought.

If you're truly passionate and truly desire to succeed in achieving your dreams, you need to be cognizant of the reasons why people quit and make a commitment to not fall victim to them. Sometimes, it's easy to quit and just walk away from your team, but this will also be an action that you take that will haunt you for the rest of your life. No matter who you are, we are only given one ticket to this voyage called life, and most of us only have less than 100 years to accomplish things while we're above ground. The more things you put off, quit, or never start will only be harder to accomplish in the future (unless there is a logical reason, and I'll address that in a moment).

Can you remember something that you've accomplished that you initially thought was impossible, and you were really close to quitting? Maybe it was a sport, maybe a time in school, or a job you were working? The situation seemed like it was just not going to happen and you were so close to throwing in the towel, but you fought just a little longer. Then it happened . . . you succeeded. What you thought was hard or impossible to accomplish actually happened and you generated success. Now when you think back about that situation, you're probably thinking "Thank God, I didn't quit!" right? Pain is temporary and if you can get through it, if you can fight past the immediate challenge, you will have earned the right to enjoy the success you generate once the task is complete. Fight through the pain and fight through the challenges in all that you're working to achieve and accomplish.

THE COST OF QUITTING

An event like this happened to me in the beginning stages of my business career. Right after I left the U.S. Navy, I needed to find employment in the civilian world. My very first job right out of the Navy was a supervisor position at Blockbuster Video. This was a really fun job, but the pay was not really enough for me to effectively pay the bills, and thus I started looking around for a higher paying job.

I saw an ad in the newspaper for a computer sales position and the advertised annual salary looked really good. I applied for the job, knowing that I was nowhere near qualified for the position, due to the fact that I knew nothing about computers and had never held a sales position before in my life. I submitted my resume knowing that I would not get a call back from the company, but less than a week later, they did call me back, and even set up a face-to-face interview. I was extremely excited about this opportunity, but in the back of my mind I knew that I was not even close to being qualified for the job, and I knew that the chance of me looking like a complete fool in front of the interviewer was a very real possibility. I was about to call and cancel the interview. I thought about it and knew that I needed to make more money to pay my bills so I stuck with it and went to the interview. During the interview, I was asked about my experience with computers and I was honest and said that I needed to learn things, but I was a quick learn and would commit to picking things up fast. I was asked, "So tell me why should I hire you then?" and here's where I knocked the ball out of the field.

I told the interviewer that while I was not going to be the most computer proficient individual that he was going to interview that day, I would be the hungriest and most determined to succeed and generate results for his company. The interviewer smiled and told me that he'd let me know soon if I got the position or not. Two days later I got the call telling me that I would be starting in two weeks.

The reason why this example is pivotal for me is because this was my first job in the computer industry and if I would not have gotten that job, I would not be where I am today. That job introduced me to computers, business, and the world of sales. Looking back, it was by far one of the most important jobs that I've had that impacted my career, and I almost quit it before I even started it.

After completing training and spending a good six months "drinking through a fire-hose" as they say, I went on to not only succeeding in selling for this company, but I became a Regional Sales Trainer and opened stores for them in the Midwest. I also trained inside and outside sales representatives how to effectively sell computers to companies and individuals. Within two years, the kid who knew absolutely nothing about computers went on to teach others about computers and about selling them. Never quit because what it is that you're working on can, and more than likely will, have a substantial positive impact on your life. The cost of quitting would have been substantial to me, and who knows the direction I would have taken with my career if I hadn't fought through the impulse to quit the steps needed to land my first professional job.

Quitting has a cost and for some the cost is substantial. Never quit on your dreams and always fight through the challenges.

WHEN YOU SHOULD QUIT

You might be confused by this heading, but there is a method to my madness here. Sometimes we start things that we never really intended to complete and never really committed our hearts and souls to completing. Personally, I have done this a number of times, but I've come to learn that this is a normal "feeling out" process that most of us experience. We think we're interested in achieving a goal or completing a task or project, but once we start, it's not really something in which we want to invest our time. If this happens, it's all right to quit and in fact you should quit as soon as you can. Any time, energy, money, or effort that you invest in anything other than the things you are truly committed to is a waste, unless you're learning something. Also, as I mentioned previously, the things you never start, put off, or quit will only be harder to complete in the future **unless** it is something that you need to gain additional experience or education with before you can complete it. The challenge with this statement is that many people will never start something because they feel that they are not 100% ready, and since 100% readiness in anything is extremely rare, they never start working towards the goal. You really have to take inventory of yourself and ensure that you're delaying the start of something purely because you need to gain additional knowledge, and you've established a clear timeline as to when you'll start the effort.

For example, let's say it was your goal to start your own business and run your own company. After doing the research, you found out that it's fairly easy to complete the required State registration for a new business; the process of incorporating a business is somewhat expensive and complex, but doable, and you have a really good idea for the type of business you'd like to start. You get excited about the possibilities of starting your new business so you visit the local SBA (Small Business Administration) office and you sit down with a guidance counselor. The first thing she asks for is a copy of your business and marketing plan. "Business and marking plan?" you ask. Ok, maybe you don't have a business and marketing plan just yet, but she then asks how you've set up your finance and accounting records for the business. "Finance and accounting records?" you mumble. Ok, so maybe you don't have a business and marketing plan or account records set up, but then she asks about business insurance, your sales plans, and your business process flows. At this point, you realize that additional training is required in order to achieve your goals, and this is a pivotal point in many people's lives. A certain percentage of people in this situation will just throw in the towel and walk away from their dream. The elements of unknown presented by this situation cause them to just kill the idea altogether. A true fighter will not walk away. Maybe the required training takes a week, maybe a year, maybe four or more years? It doesn't matter to the fighter because owning a business is the dream for this person and they will do whatever it takes to achieve this goal and generate success.

Another example of when it is acceptable to quit is when you find yourself involved in something that you thought was legitimate and honest, but you later find out this is not the case. An example of this happened to me when I was younger and looking for ways to increase my level of income. I found out about a multi-level marketing company that was selling products good for the environment, and in the process, people selling the products were reportedly making thousands and thousands of dollars. To me this seemed like a win-win situation, because not only could I sell something that generated benefits for people, I'd have an opportunity to make six-figures or more. I attended an introduction meeting for the company and it seemed like a great deal. The representatives for the company were energetic, the local sales representatives were all pumped up, and the product looked good. All I had to do was invest $5,000 in the product and then start to promote the product, as well as bring in additional people who might be interested in making more money themselves.

The investment of $5,000 was huge for me at the time because I didn't really have the money and would have to put it on a credit card, but I figured that if I was serious about success, I needed to put some skin in the game. I purchased my inventory and started placing ads in the local newspaper to start developing my sales team. I was then told that if I really wanted to be successful at the company, I needed to attend a national sales conference in Detroit. At this point, I was heavy in debt with the company, so what was a couple of hundred dollars?

I invested in the seminar and drove up to Detroit. At the sales event, I started to see the company in a different light. I started to see that there was a lot of hype to get people in the company and for them to invest in their inventory, but hardly anyone was making money from selling the product. At the seminar we were told that you have to create a false personality of success and that we should "fake it till we make it" in order to be successful. This didn't seem right to me and so when I returned to my local sales office I started to look around to see who was really making money and who was "faking it till they made it," and it was then that I saw no one was making any money. It was all smoke and mirrors and a situation where people were lied to in order to get additional people to join the pyramid scheme. I immediately quit the company, but this was really a negative experience for me because I'd made a stupid mistake investing my money and it also caused me to doubt my business and selling skills. It took me several months to recoup from that situation, but after the wounds had healed I saw this as the incredible opportunity of education that it was for me. In life you learn from the great things that you do, as well as the stuff that you mess up in the process. For me, this was a mistake but I learned that I should always trust my gut, question everything, and that unless I believe 100% in something, I can't sell anything. I also learned to look at the details, and if something is not honest and legitimate, get the heck out of it.

The final situation when it makes sense to quit is when you've generated the level of success that you've worked to accomplish, and it's time to call it a day. You came, you saw, you kicked butt, as they say. An example of this in MMA occurred in 2010 when one of the heroes of the sport, Chuck Liddell, announced his retirement. Chuck's professional record of 21 wins, 8 losses, and 0 draws, and included incredible fights with opponents such as Wanderlei Silva, Quinton Jackson, Tito Ortiz, and Randy Couture, just to name a few warriors he fought. Even before retiring from the sport, Chuck was named to the UFC hall-of-fame and has been an iconic figure of the sport since the beginning of the UFC's rise to fame. Chuck is a former UFC World Light Heavy Weight champion and his knock outs have frequented highlight reels for many years now. Chuck is the real example of someone who kicked much ass, took many names, and established a legendary name for himself in the process. Dana White, UFC President, once said about Chuck that, "He has nothing else to prove. He is the most famous Mixed Martial Artist on the planet, he's made more money than God, he's a champion and he's got nothing else to fight for."(25)

Chuck's impact on the UFC and MMA has been so substantial that in 2011 Dana White announced that Chuck had been hired as the Vice President of Business Development for Zuffa LLC. Remember, quitting is the last thing you want to do, but in some cases it makes sense as long as there is a legitimate and logical reason for stopping the activity or task that you're doing, or if like Chuck Liddell, you generated the success you set out to accomplish and now it's time to achieve success in something new.

THE POWER OF PERSEVERANCE

The great motivator and author Napoleon Hill once said, "Before success comes in any man's life, he's sure to meet with much temporary defeat and, perhaps some failures. When defeat overtakes a man, the easiest and the most logical thing to do is to quit. That's exactly what the majority of men do." Perseverance is the ability to maintain action and the intestinal fortitude to continue fighting to achieve something that you've been working to accomplish. Many people are blessed with uncanny perseverance, and some people quit things the minute it becomes hard for them. The challenge with many goals and dreams is that most of the time we're not completely sure how much more work or effort is required to generate the success for which we're striving. It literally might be just another hour of work, or it might require most of one's life to achieve a milestone. If something is truly important to a fighter, he or she will work for however long it takes. It becomes critical to their life and day to day living.

This topic reminds me of a story I once heard about two frogs that got stuck in a jar of milk. The first frog jumped several times but it could not clear the top of the jar. The other yelled that the frog should keep trying, so the frog jumped two more times but still failed to clear the jar. Frustrated and positive that it was doomed, the frog sank to the bottom of the jar and died. The remaining frog did not give it. It jumped and jumped for hours on end.

The frog became tired but it did not stop jumping because it knew that it was strong enough to clear the jar, it just had to keep working.

All of a sudden because of the frog's constant jumping, the milk turned to butter and the remaining frog was able to jump out to its freedom. The frog that perished had allowed the elements of the unknown to frustrate it and it gave up. The frog that turned the milk to butter kept going on and relied on his belief that he would succeed to carry him through the process.

The sport of MMA is a beacon to those who have a passion for working hard, are driven, persistent to the extreme, and who live life to its full and true potential. An example of this type of personality can be found with Kyle Maynard. Kyle was born without arms below his elbows or legs below his knees, and yet he wrestled in high school, as well as competed in MMA in 2009. While the norm will come up with excuse after excuse as to why they can't run a marathon, mountain climb, bike 100 miles, or even get themselves off the couch and into the gym, you have warriors like Kyle that do what some men with arms and legs fear to attempt. Kyle doesn't even look at his situation as a disadvantage and was quoted as saying, "I think I've been given an advantage. I think I've been given an unfair advantage to get the most out of life".(26)

The people who are the most persistent and utilize perseverance with effectiveness are normally the people who deploy a system that allows them to remain aware of what they're working towards, as well as what they've completed to date.

Activities and accomplishments have a tendency to become forgotten over time and what you've completed to date might actually amaze you if you monitor your progress and occasionally review your accomplishments. People who are serious about working out in the gym will normally log their target workout, as well as actual results, to ensure they are generating the level of activity they feel is required to hit a fitness goal. All of your activities, goals, and required steps of activity can actually be logged in this same fashion. Your log does not have to be anything fancy, and I've even used a single sheet of paper that included the basic scribbles of what I wanted to complete during a day's activity or a work out session. What's key is that you keep track of your progress so you can start to measure your results. Once you see yourself progressing in a given area it will motivate you further and fuel your intensity to get even better. Think of the weight lifter who wants to bench press 230 pounds. Every day when he hits the gym he takes with him a log of exercises he will complete, as well as the number of sets and repetitions that he will complete per exercise. He'll visualize the days he's achieved or exceeded his expectations, as well as the days where perhaps he failed to complete what he wanted to accomplish. He'll keep his ultimate goal listed at the top of his daily logs: bench press 230 pounds in 30 days. He works his plan day after day and then something happens on day 21; he bench presses 230 pounds. His goal was achieved before he expected it, and not only is he proud of his accomplishment; he's now jacked out of his mind with motivation and knowledge that he can do even better. He sets his next goal of benching 245 pounds within the next 30 days, and the cycle begins again.

CREATING YOUR ACCOMPLISHMENT LOG

As mentioned above, successful people keep track of their progress and accomplishments. One of the best ways to avoid quitting and to always fuel your persistence is to know that you CAN complete a task and have generated accomplishments while working towards your goals. The best way to track your progress is to log your activities while you're working on them and then store this data into a computer, ideally within a software program such as Microsoft Excel. The reason why this is helpful is because with Excel you can use your raw data and then create graphs that will allow you to visually track your results. If you're a visual person like I am, this is a very helpful process towards completing goals. If you don't have a computer, then just maintain a journal book and keep the data logged in a fashion that best resonates with you. There isn't a wrong or right way to do something like this, but there certainly are easy and effective ways to track data, and as long as the data is useful for you, that's all that counts. Also, I purposely call this an Accomplishment Log versus something like a Work Log or Activity Tracker. To me, an Accomplishment Log has a positive ring to it, and again we're all striving to accomplish things and not just do more work or take on more tasks.

To create your Accomplishment Log, you should do the following:

1.) Create your master file within Excel or purchase a binder with paper at your local office supplies store. If you have a computer and will be creating a master Accomplishment Log on your computer, still purchase a binder or a book with blank paper so you can use this during your actual training (unless you take your computer with you at all times).

2.) Within your data file or binder, write down your "why" statement. Remember, as we discussed in Chapter Two, at the heart of achieving any goal in life is understanding why you're doing something, what's at stake if you lose, and what you will gain when you win.

3.) Next, write down the activities that you are required to complete on a daily, weekly, or monthly basis in order to achieve your targeted goal.

4.) Then, write down the individual tasks that must be completed per item. For example, if you're creating a work out chart and you're listing the exercises that you'll need to complete, write down how many repetitions and sets you'll have to accomplish per workout.

5.) Additionally, add a space for comments. You will use this space to write about the specific item. Perhaps it's a comment about how you thought the exercise was easier than you'd thought it would be, or why you weren't able to complete the full sets. This data will later help you adjust your work out regimens for greater effectiveness.

6.) Take your Accomplishment Log with you as you train or begin working on your goals.

7.) After completing your tasks and logging your data in your book, log this data into your master Accomplishment Log file.

8.) Track and use your data to monitor your progress and achievement.

9.) Adjust your master Accomplishment Log and data binder/ book as your goals are achieved.

For purposes of example, below is what an Accomplishment Log and data binder/book might look like. To remain consistent, I'll use the example of our weight lifter who was working to achieve the goal of benching 230 pounds in eight weeks or less.

Daily Accomplishment Log

Why: Benching 230 pounds will allow me to gain muscle mass and increase my strength, thus helping me in football.
Being the best at football is critical to me because I want to play for the NFL in less than 5 years.

WorkOut Regiment

	Sets	Reps	Weight	Comments:
Bench	6	8	205	First two sets were fine. Struggled on the last four.
Incline	6	8	125	Shoulders hurt a little so I went light today
Decline	6	8	210	Decline felt good. I'm moving to 225 next time.
Flys	5	8	70	Pulled on shoulders a little. Backed off on the last two sets.
Plyo Push	10	20	NA	Felt good and I see results from this exercise.
Shrugs	6	8	80	Felt good. I think I can move to 85 pounds next time.

Weekly Accomplishment Log:

Why: Benching 230 pounds will allow me to gain muscle mass and increase my strength, thus helping me in football.

Being the best at football is critical to me because I want to play for the NFL in less than 5 years.

Results

	Week 1	Week 2	Week 3	Week 4	Week 5	Week 6	Week 7	Week 8
Bench	205	205	210	210	210	225	225	230

Week 1 Notes: Started out benching 205 pounds. Weight is fairly easy to lift.

Week 2: Stayed at 205 pounds for a bench max this week. Increased my protein intake after working out.

Week 3: Benched 210 pounds! Awesome, and the weight felt good.

Week 4: Stayed at 210 pounds this week. Weight felt good but I couldn't move up. Increased protein intake.

Week 5: Stuck at 210 pounds this week, but did an awesome burn out set where I benched 205 pounds 10 times.

Week 6: Yes! Benched 225 pounds. I'm almost at 230 pounds.

Week 7: Stayed at 225 pounds. I still feel confident I'll hit 230 pounds by the end of next week.

Week 8: Hit it!! Benched 230 pounds. It was hard but I pushed it out. Here I come 250 pounds.

THE PRIMAL POWER OF NOT QUITTING

You've seen it hundreds of times while watching television shows about animals in the wild. There is always an alpha-male in every pride, flock, or herd. The alpha-male is the animal with the power and the balls to take control over the rest of the animals within his group. The alpha-male feeds first, mates with his choice of females, and ensures that the general situation within the pride is to his liking. Pretty nice gig, huh? The thing is, the alpha-male is constantly challenged by younger males within and outside of the pride who feel they are more powerful and ready to take over the group. If the alpha-male quits during a fight and submits to the opposing force, if he is not killed, he will be demoted to now follow this stronger male, or potentially even be driven from the group altogether.

Another example of the primal power of not quitting can be seen when a lion or a cheetah hunts for food. We've all seen footage of the cheetah chasing the gazelle and the race seems to go on forever. The gazelle darts back and forth at great speed, but the cheetah continues to track it. Finally, with one small wrong turn, the gazelle slips and the cheetah pounces. Food is rewarded to the cheetah. If he would have quit the pursuit, the alternative would have meant hunger and weakness, which would result in other potential challenges if this cheetah was later forced to fight or protect its cubs.

Quitting has an impact on nature, whether we're talking about humans or animals. Every day, whether you realize it or not, you're fighting for your food, shelter, and position in life.

You're fighting to ensure what you've earned is maintained and what you cherish is protected. In some cases if you slip, just like the gazelle, the ramifications you encounter will be fierce and immediate. The world of business is literally dog-eat-dog at times; the world of athletics is measured by your dominance over another human or group of humans; the world of academics is full of people who are working to score higher than the person next to them. While this might sound a little ominous, this fact of life is also an incredible motivator for those who recognize its primal power. Deep inside all of us, we are that animal who wants to be the alpha-male (or alpha-female for you ladies), who will fight when engaged, and who understands the ways of the world, but will use these conditions to fuel the motivation to grow, gain, and prosper. Now this does not mean that you have to start wearing a crown or drafting your plot for world domination, but it does mean that you should always be cognizant of what's at stake in your life, what's threatened, and understand the ramifications of quitting the fight that you're in while working to gain success and protect what is rightfully yours. Remember this when times get tough, and they will get tough, when you're challenged to fight for what you're working to accomplish. When you're exhausted and perhaps questioning your own sanity, don't quit! Keep fighting and realize that when you've accomplished your goals and generated the success you are destined to achieve, it will all be worth it in the end.

DON'T QUIT CREED

When things go wrong as they sometimes will;
When the road you're trudging seems all uphill;
When the funds are low, and the debts are high;
And you want to smile, but you have to sigh;
When care is pressing you down a bit-
Rest if you must, but don't you quit.
Success is failure turned inside out;
The silver tint of the clouds of doubt;
And you can never tell how close you are;
It may be near when it seems afar.
So, stick to the fight when you're hardest hit—
It's when things go wrong that you mustn't quit.(52)
Author Unknown

RULES OF THE OCTAGON

Rule #4: Never quit until you've achieved success

If what you're pursuing is truly something that you're passionate about, physically and mentally ready to receive, and something you're totally set on accomplishing, never quit. As mentioned before, there will be times when you're challenged beyond any level that you have ever expected to be challenged on, but he/she who fights past challenges and adversity enjoys the spoils of success. Effective techniques for maintaining the tenacity and motivation you'll need to get past the obstacles and issues you might experience include:

- Always remember your "why" and keep your why statement in front of you at all times.
- Understand that most things are temporary and finite. As the saying goes "this too shall pass" and as long as you don't quit, you'll get past the rough times.
- Measure and track your progress and use your accomplishments and successes to fuel your motivation and tenacity. Use what you achieve to drive motivation for additional growth.
- Understand that not only is character built during hard times, but our challenges expand our skills, strengths, and confidence as we overcome them.
- Understand that there's a reason for most things and while you might not immediately understand why you have to face a challenge, you'll later clearly understand the lesson, as well as what you gained during the experience.

THE SCORECARD

- *NEVER QUIT ANYTHING YOU'RE PASSIONATE ABOUT; BE READY TO RECEIVE IT, AND 100% READY TO FIGHT TO ACHIEVE IT*
- *IF YOU'RE NOT PASSIONATE, NOT FULLY READY, OR NOT WILLING TO GIVE SOMETHING 100%, GET OUT QUICK SO YOU DON'T WASTE YOUR TIME*
- *PAIN IS TEMPORARY BUT FAILURE CAN BE FOREVER*
- *REMEMBER THAT SOME GOALS AND AMBITIONS REQUIRE ADDITIONAL SKILLS AND TRAINING, SO GAIN WHAT EXPERIENCE YOU NEED BUT DON'T USE THIS AS AN EXCUSE TO QUIT*
- *TRACK AND MEASURE YOUR PROGRESS. USE YOUR ACCOMPLISHMENTS AS FUEL TO GAIN MORE SUCCESS*

Chapter 5

Dedication, Passion, and Focus on Success

"I told them to find what they are passionate about and to go for that regardless of what anyone tells them. They can go to school and major in political science and say they want to be a doctor or a lawyer, but unless they're passionate about what they do, they're never really going to be happy or truly successful." Dana White(27)

A WHOLE NEW LEVEL OF MEASUREMENT

Most sports require a degree of dedication and commitment from the athletes that participate in them, but the sport of mixed martial arts takes dedication, passion, and focus to a whole new level. Many of the athletes who participate in MMA train multiple times a day, and then escalate their level of training even further when they begin preparing for a bout. MMA is such a dynamic and physical sport, and one that generates incredible fitness results for its practitioners. Today, many gyms are offering MMA classes just to help average people lose weight and get in shape.

Results generated in MMA, like business, school, and life in general, are in direct proportion to the amount of effort, dedication, and focus an individual is willing to offer. Some people are willing to give everything to be successful. They are willing to endure whatever life will throw at them in order to achieve results.

UFC fighter George Sotiropoulos is an example of a fighter dedicated to mastering his craft. George has traveled all over the world, visiting gym after gym to learn from as many coaches and instructors as possible. The unique element to this story is that George did this world travel with very little money and had to sleep on hard gym floors at night, and work odd jobs to secure whatever money he could in order to eat and continue his training. Today, George is a serious up-and-comer in the 155 pound lightweight weight class.

Now you might be thinking to yourself that you've heard hundreds of similar stories about people who have gone through extremely rough times in order to achieve a dream or accomplish a life mission, and I would tell you that you're absolutely right. You can probably also think of hundreds of examples where you've seen people not even complete the first step towards success and stop doing a task because it was too hard or subjected them to difficulties. The difference between those who achieve success and those who don't is their level of dedication, passion, and tenacity. A success-oriented individual will do whatever is required to achieve success, and endure whatever challenges that are thrown their way in the process. Those truly oriented toward success also have a tendency towards escalating their level of dedication, passion, and focus to a scale that some might call intense or even radical. In the sport of MMA, for example, a fighter must make a certain weight before being allowed to fight. If the fighter does not make weight, he or she will either be disqualified or will face the potential of other financial and/or fight penalties.

Making weight for some fighters is an intense and painful process that can involve a fighter dropping as much as twenty or more pounds just a few weeks before a fight. The process of losing the weight involves intense cardiovascular exercises, adhering to a regimented diet, and in many cases, reducing massive amounts of water weight by sitting in heated saunas while wearing a sweat suit. Several episodes of the reality show *The Ultimate Fighter* on Spike TV have offered scenes where fighters had to endure sauna sessions that in many cases left people begging to be let out of the heated room.

In many cases they were not let out because they were overweight and their teammates were there to remind them of what was at stake if they came out and did not lose the weight. When they did come out, large amounts of water poured out of their sweat suits as they removed their clothes. Some might call this intense, but it's what many fighters have to endure in order to be prepared and be in a position to compete and complete what they are working to achieve. This same degree of intensity might be found in the student that pulls an "all-nighter" to prepare for a test, the doctor that works 24 hours on, 24 hours off at a hospital, the fire-fighter that dives in the middle of a house completely engulfed in flames. Intensity resides in all of us, and is like a sleeping dragon. It will lie dormant and quiet but once it's awoken, its existence will be immediately known. Intensity is made up of three components: dedication, passion, and focus. Dedication, passion, and focus are three key and critical elements to success and anyone armed with these three ingredients of achievement will be well positioned to win and accomplish what they are seeking to achieve.

DEDICATION

The historic Iberian military general, Tariq Ibn Ziyad, understood dedication. Legend has it that in the year 711, Ziyad and his army invaded and conquered the Visigothic Kingdom (modern day Spain and Portugal), but what was amazing about this conquest was not the victory as much as it was the manner in which Ziyad displayed dedication to the battle. The way that Ziyad ensured that he, as well as his warriors, devoted 100% to the efforts of victory or death was by burning their ships when they landed on the North coast of Morocco.

Before the battle started, Ziyad had their vessels burned and with the ships aflame in the background, he gave a speech to his men that began with, "Oh, my warriors, whither would you flee? Behind you is the sea, before you, the enemy. You have left now only the hope of your courage and your constancy. Remember that in this country you are more unfortunate than the orphan seated at the table of the avaricious master. Your enemy is before you, protected by an innumerable army; he has men in abundance, but you, as your only aid, have your own swords, and, as your only chance for life, such chance as you can snatch from the hands of your enemy. If the absolute want to which you are reduced is prolonged ever so little, if you delay to seize immediate success, your good fortune will vanish, and your enemies, whom your very presence has filled with fear, will take courage. Put far from you the disgrace from which you flee in dreams, and attack this monarch who has left his strongly fortified city to meet you. Here is a splendid opportunity to defeat him, if you will consent to expose yourselves freely to death.

Do not believe that I desire to incite you to face dangers which I shall refuse to share with you. In the attack I myself will be in the fore, where the chance of life is always least."(28)

Ziyad created a do or die situation for his men and mentally conditioned them to understand that they either conquered the enemy or they would die trying to achieve this effort. Ziyad created the conditioning needed to ensure victory in battle. It is also said that the Spanish conqueror, Hector Cortez, burned his ships when he invaded Central America, and legend has it that ancient Vikings burned their vessels when they launched battles against adversaries. While the stories and legends related to the burning of boats varies and is debated by many historians, the concept is solid. If you're dedicated enough to subject yourself to a win or die trying situation, you will come to the game prepared to let it all go and fight until victory is achieved. There are no alternatives other than elimination. It is all about proper mental conditioning.

T.K.O. (Tips, Knowledge, and Objectives)

Burn your boats but don't burn your bridges. Something that I learned early in my career is that it's not only what you know that can take you far, it's also who you know. Sometimes the "who you know" is even more important than the "what you know." When you decide to make a leap of faith in life and hang it all out there in your do or die situation, just make sure you don't damage or destroy relationships in the process. I've seen so many examples where bridges were burnt and these relationships later became critical to one's success. Set ablaze your trail of success, but never burn your bridges.

Former UFC middleweight champion Frank Shamrock once said that, "Conditioning is my best weapon."(29) Conditioning, or the preparations that one takes to ensure they are physically and mentally prepared for battle, is the best weapon for anyone working to achieve success. The level of dedication and commitment to conditioning is also a tangible differentiator of those who achieve radical success, compared to those who just achieve moderate success or don't succeed at all. Conditioning complimented with intense dedication creates unstoppable force for success and achievement.

UFC fighter Ben Henderson once said that, "To win a fight, it takes a sincere dedication to prepare for that fight as completely and fully as possible. There should be no doubt in your heart that you did everything possible to be prepared. I always use taking a test in high school as an analogy. For most kids in high school, they get a little apprehensive before tests because they know they should have and could have studied for it a little better, a little more. Now say you study the test material for literally three hours a night for a solid month and in your heart of hearts you know you could not have studied any better or longer, then that little bit of doubt goes away going into the test. I use this analogy because most people know exactly how it feels to not have studied enough for a test in high school and exactly how it feels to be utterly unconcerned for a test because you are 100% prepared. The real kicker to getting and being prepared could be 180 degrees different for what it takes another fighter to feel the same. It's a process that all fighters have to work through to learn what the best is for them.

I use the test taking analogy because sometimes you can be completely prepared for the test and there's no trepidation, but you flunk the test because it's just too hard. It's the same way in fighting. Sometimes no matter how prepared you are for the fight, the other guy is better on that night. The only thing you can do is keep your head up and begin preparations for the next one and hopefully be able to refine your preparations."(30)

Another example of the level of dedication in the sport of MMA can be found with UFC fighter Nate Quarry. Nate had degenerative disc disease and severe back pain to the point where even holding his daughter was a struggle. It was improbable that Nate would continue to fight within the sport of MMA, and most men in his position wouldn't have even considered the idea of continuing to fight. Dedication to the sport he loved kicked in and Nate discovered a new spinal procedure called Extreme Lateral Interbody Fusion that allowed his surgeon to insert a stabilizing implant into his back. The results of the procedure were profound. Not only was his back pain gone, but Nate was allowed to continue his fighting career with dominant fashion. The average man would have stopped fighting after the surgery, or perhaps wouldn't have endured the surgery, but Nate is an example of dedication in action, and is a force far from average.(31)

The level of dedication that you exhibit to key components of success, such as preparation and perspiration, is in direct proportion to the progress you make towards prosperity.

PASSION

The French philosopher Denis Diderot once said, "Only passions, great passions can elevate the soul to great things."(32) Passion is the root that makes the plant of success grow into a powerful tree. Without passion, even the most talented person will never achieve their full potential or accomplish all that they could have accomplished in their lifetime. If you want to see passion in action, watch any interview of UFC President Dana White, or listen to any fight covered by ring announcers Joe Rogan and Mike Goldberg. The passion that these gentlemen display for the sport of MMA and their position within the UFC is intense and energetic, to make an understatement. If you're passionate about what you're doing in life, people will see this and your attitude will be infectious. People will want to know more about what you're doing and be part of the experience.

One of my favorite Latin phrases is "carpe diem," which means "seize the day." People who are passionate about what they are working to achieve in life realize the importance and benefit of seizing the day. They live with intense energy and do as much as one can do to squeeze every ounce of life that they're allotted in a 24 hour period. Life offers us so many gifts on a daily basis, and unfortunately, many people only choose to focus on the dread and not the dynamics of our existence. When you live with passion everything around you will be enhanced.

Additional opportunities will open up for you because, as mentioned previously, people will want to be around you and support you, but in addition to that, passionate people do more thus creating additional avenues of action where average people only see closed doors. Think about it this way, no matter who you are, we're each only allotted 24 hours in a day, seven days during a week, and maybe, if we're lucky, a good 85-100 years on this Earth. Our time is finite. Every second you spend doing something you're not passionate about, is gone. Obviously, there are things that we have to do in life that we may not be passionate about at all, but they're required in order to function as a human and exist within a society, but I think you understand my point here. If you work a job that does not make you happy, stay in a relationship that is unfulfilling, or spend your day doing monotonous tasks that just pass the time, this time is gone. Imagine how it would be if every morning you woke up and couldn't wait to start your day. The thought of getting another day to live just jazzes you up with energy and passion. You never go to work; you go to the place or do the thing that makes you happy, but also happens to generate wealth for you. You appreciate everything around you and you show your appreciation.

Showing appreciation is an effective way of triggering and activating your passion. Every day most of us wake up with incredible gifts such as sight, hearing, the ability to walk, and talk. We're blessed with health, wealth (and if you don't agree with me on this one, Google poverty in Africa and then tell me you're not wealthy), and the desire for greater success. Unfortunately, many don't realize these gifts until they no longer have them.

Imagine how valuable the ability to walk is for a man or woman who does not have legs or is paralyzed? Imagine how it would be if you could no longer see or speak? Yes, these are depressing thoughts, but even more depressing would be to lose one of these gifts and only at that time realize what you had and fully appreciate the wonderful things we are granted on a daily basis. Every day, before I pick up the phone or turn on the computer to start my day, I say a prayer of appreciation. I'm not the most religious person that you'll run into, but I do believe in God and I believe in the old saying that "what you think about, thank about, you bring about." I believe that God is the source of what created the Earth and the things around us. I also believe that we should show appreciation for all that we have and when I pray, I don't ask for anything, I just thank God for what I have. I think that everyone should have their own prayer of appreciation, but if you want to use the prayer that I use every day, it goes as such:

Prayer of Appreciation

Dear God, thank you for yesterday, today, and tomorrow. Thank you for protecting, guiding, and being with myself and my family. Thank you for this planet and the people on this Earth. Thank you for the peace that we have and the additional peace that we gain on a daily basis. Thank you for my health, my wealth, and my success. Thank you for allowing today to be lucrative, prosperous, fun, entertaining, and full of love and adventure. Thank you for allowing me to connect with people, laugh, and make the most out of my day. Thank you for allowing my day to be rewarding and free from stress. Thank you for everything that I have. I appreciate everything that I have and I'm thankful for everything that you've done for me and my family. Thank you! Amen

As you can see, my prayer of appreciation is relatively simple and straightforward, but who said things have to be difficult and complex? Just show appreciation for what you have and what you'll gain in the future and watch what happens to you in your life. Your passion backed by appreciation is a formula for great success.

FOCUS

Focus is the application of concentration, effort, and energy needed to generate results. It is also the glue that holds together the frame of success that dedication and passion create for an individual. Focus is critical to success no matter what endeavor one works to achieve in life. For some, focus is as simple of shifting energy and thought onto a topic or situation until a goal is achieved. For others, focus involves a shifting of lifestyle, making sacrifices, and becoming a laser-beam of concentration on a single item, be it training or intense activity. UFC fighter Lyota Machinda once said, "I study my opponent and am so focused on them by fight time, their strikes appear to come at me in slow motion."(33) Applied focus allows an individual to be aggressive and accurate with their planning and preparation.

Focused fighters do things such as watch videos of their opponents' previous fights over and over again. They look for critical areas of weakness and habits that expose their opponents' mistakes on which they can then capitalize. Focused fighters review their own techniques to identify areas that need to be improved. They then use this focus to review their opponents and discover where they need to modify their approach to best defuse their opponents' areas of strength and expand their areas of weakness.

In business, this degree of focus comes in the shape of analytics such as target market analysis, S.W.O.T. (strength, weakness, opportunities, and threat) reports, sales pipeline management, profit and loss reviews, and market industry projections. A business without focus is like a ship without a navigational system. It may float for a while, but the chances of ever hitting goals or destinations, is slim to none. In academics, this focus comes in the form of the intensity for which one studies. It is the concentration on a specific area of coverage or major, as well as added learning scenarios such as study groups, tutoring, and seminar attendance.

While focus is mostly a positive element of success, it is also a complicated component that can generate negative results. As we learned in the "Invisible Gorilla" experiment covered in Chapter three, applied focus without holistic or complete surrounding awareness can actually prevent you from seeing the complete picture or life scenario.

Fighters capitalize from applied focus without holistic awareness. A technique that I learned while studying karate involved watching your opponent's eyes and when he/she starts to focus on your legs because they are expecting a kick, you fake a straight groin kick. Almost always, your opponent will drop both of their hands to block this incoming kick, and while their hands are down in the block position, you strike their open head with a fist punch. Focus is most powerful when you are locked on your eventual goal or target, but you're also aware of the conditions and environment of your complete surrounding. Like the old saying goes, you have to be able to see the forest for the trees.

If not, life will throw you a punch in the jaw when you're just trying to avoid what you thought was a kick to the groin.

Another potential challenge with intense focus is some people get so focused on the end result or goal, that they skip the important steps that need to be completed in the process. This can happen in fighting when a fighter looks past an immediate opponent because they are focused on eventually fighting for a championship belt. They are focused on the champion to the point that they don't pay attention (or enough attention) to their next opponent and they lose. In business, this would be like trying to win a major account while completely ignoring your current client base. I've seen it happen multiple times where sales people are so focused on winning new business that they lose their complete customer base in the process. When they don't win the new "whale account" they are left with nothing.

Effective focus takes into account the big picture, but also the small details or steps that need to be taken in order to get to the final goal. In the military, this is known as attention to detail, and its part of how a soldier or a sailor is measured when it comes to performance reviews. Optimizing focus by deploying holistic awareness and micro-level management of the required steps needed to complete tasks leading to an eventual goal is effective in generating solid results.

He or she who fully embraces, deploys, and masters dedication, passion, and focus, is a dangerous individual. This is a person who can accomplish almost anything. As an employer, this is the type of person you want working on your team and helping you to achieve your work goals and efforts.

This is the kind of person that when you meet them, you immediately feel and sense their intensity and power. They inspire other people. They are the real movers and shakers of the world. And now, armed with this knowledge, you will embody this power and intensity and generate the success you are looking to accomplish in life.

RULES OF THE OCTAGON

Rule #5: Activate and energize your dedication, passion, and focus to generate greater results and success.

Step One—Write down your goals and desired accomplishments: This data was already captured in the previous chapters, so just add the goals and objectives you've documented to this point. If you have less than five goals, simply add what you have. If you have more than five goals, document them on a separate sheet of paper.

Goal #1: _____

Goal #2: _____

Goal #3: _____

Goal #4: _____

Goal #5: _____

Step Two—Identify your level of dedication: For me, I know that I'm the type of person who has to be fully dedicated to the thing I'm working to complete. If not, my interest wanders and I move on to the next thing, but if I'm dedicated to a task or goal, it WILL get done. Regarding the goals that you listed above, how dedicated are you to accomplishing them?

Goal #1:   Dedication Level 1-10 (10 being the highest)

_____   _____

Goal #2:   Dedication Level 1-10 (10 being the highest)

_____   _____

Goal #3:   Dedication Level 1-10 (10 being the highest)

_____   _____

Goal #4:   Dedication Level 1-10 (10 being the highest)

_____   _____

Goal #5:   Dedication Level 1-10 (10 being the highest)

_____   _____

If you answered "10" on all of your goals, congratulations, but let's test your dedication a little. Would you still answer 10 on these goals if it meant that you would have to go without pay for a year, not see your family for six months, and live in the most modest of conditions? Think about it. If you still answered "10" then these goals are important to you.

If your answer changed to "5" or below, you still might want to pursue the goal, but it now shows that the goal is really not something you're fully committed to completing. This is ok, because we all work on things that would be nice to complete, but they're not REQUIRED to complete. A "10" dedication goal is something you HAVE to complete or else. If you answered "10," you're going to accomplish the goal or bust your ass trying.

Step Three—Identify your level of passion: How passionate are you about your goals and desired accomplishments? An easy way to answer this question is to ask someone close to you what they think you're most passionate about. If they answer with something that is related to your goals, then you're on track. If they don't know or if they answer with something other than your goals, you might need to step it up. When a person is passionate about their goals, almost everyone they come into contact with is aware of what they are working to accomplish. People can literally feel your passion as you speak about the goal you're working to complete.

This energy is infectious and you'll find that once people sense this from you, they will want to help you achieve your goals as well. People want to be part of something and really want to be part of something that is successful and big.

Goal #1:   Level of Passion 1-10 (10 being the highest)

_____   _____

Goal #2:   Level of Passion 1-10 (10 being the highest)

_____   _____

Goal #3:   Level of Passion 1-10 (10 being the highest)

_____   _____

Goal #4:   Level of Passion 1-10 (10 being the highest)

_____   _____

Goal #5:   Level of Passion 1-10 (10 being the highest)

_____   _____

Again, if you answered "10" to the goals above, ask people close to you if they agree with your assessment, or ask yourself when the last time was that you remember really being stoked about the goal. If you find that you're constantly thinking about the goal and constantly eating, breathing, living, and sleeping the goal, then you're passionate about it.

Step Four—Identify your level of focus: How focused are you on your goals and objectives? If you were able to write down your goals at the beginning of this exercise, then it at least shows me that you have a degree of holistic awareness of these goals. If you struggled to identify your goals, then we have some work to do.

As we discussed in Chapter one, you have to define and set your plans. Without a plan, you're simply living on hope and chance, and this rarely generates success. To ensure you have the proper degree of focus on your goals and objectives, I've created the following checklist that you can utilize to gauge your degree of focus and progress awareness.

- **Goal #1**:_____
- **Start date**:_____
- **Overall result of accomplishing the goal**:_____
- **What are the steps needed to complete the goal:**

1_____

2_____

3_____

4_____

5_____

- **What obstacles or challenges might be experienced while working to complete the goal and how will I overcome them:**

	Challenge:	Resolution:
1:	_____	_____
2:	_____	_____
3:	_____	_____

- **End date**:_____

- **Goal #2**:_____
- **Start date**:_____
- **Overall result of accomplishing the goal**:_____
- **What are the steps needed to complete the goal:**

1_____

2_____

3_____

4_____

5_____

- **What obstacles or challenges might be experienced while working to complete the goal and how will I overcome them:**

  Challenge: Resolution:

1:_____   _____

2:_____   _____

3:_____   _____

- **End date**:_____

- **Goal #3**:_____
- **Start date**:_____
- **Overall result of accomplishing the goal**:_____
- **What are the steps needed to complete the goal:**

1_____

2_____

3_____

4_____

5_____

- **What obstacles or challenges might be experienced while working to complete the goal and how will I overcome them:**

      Challenge: Resolution:

1:_____ _____

2:_____ _____

3:_____ _____

- **End date**:_____

- **Goal #4**:_____
- **Start date**:_____
- **Overall result of accomplishing the goal**:_____
- **What are the steps needed to complete the goal:**

1_____

2_____

3_____

4_____

5_____

- **What obstacles or challenges might be experienced while working to complete the goal and how will I overcome them:**

	Challenge:	Resolution:
1:	_____	_____
2:	_____	_____
3:	_____	_____

- **End date**:_____

- **Goal #5:**_____
- **Start date:**_____
- **Overall result of accomplishing the goal:**_____
- **What are the steps needed to complete the goal:**

1_____

2_____

3_____

4_____

5_____

- **What obstacles or challenges might be experienced while working to complete the goal and how will I overcome them:**

          Challenge: Resolution:

1:_____   _____

2:_____   _____

3:_____   _____

- **End date:**_____

THE SCORECARD

- *COMMIT TO A DEGREE OF DEDICATION THAT GOES BEYOND THE NORM*
- *CONDITION YOURSELF FOR OPTIMUM SUCCESS*
- *POSSESS A TRUE PASSION FOR WHAT YOU'RE LOOKING TO ACCOMPLISH IN LIFE*
- *APPLY THE NECESSARY DEGREE OF FOCUS THAT IT TAKES TO ACCOMPLISH YOUR GOALS AND ACHIEVE SUCCESS*
- *FOCUS ON THE BIG PICTURE, AS WELL AS THE INDIVIDUAL STEPS THAT IT WILL TAKE TO COMPLETE YOUR OBJECTIVES*

Chapter 6

Leadership

"I think that everyone is capable of being a leader when given a chance." Dana White (34)

THE IMPORTANCE OF LEADERSHIP

Effective leadership is critical in practically every facet of life. Regardless if we're discussing business, politics, or sports, leaders within organizations are key figures that make things work, or become the root cause of why things fail. In the world of mixed martial arts, results-based and forward-thinking leadership is vital due to the fact that the sport is growing substantially and is still relatively new. Successful leadership will take MMA to the next level of gaining an even larger fan base, expanding coverage of media attention, as well as increasing the awareness and future creation of events that will take place globally.

Leadership is important because it is the foundation that sets the path and direction for an organization or group. Leadership also defines the vision that others follow. Leadership establishes and fuels the passion and motivation that helps an organization or group maintain the course during the good times and the bad times. If a leader falls, it has an impact on the organization or group as a whole, as well as on how others outside of the group view the effectiveness of the organization.

An example of successful leadership within MMA can be found with Dana White, President of the UFC. Before becoming the President of the largest MMA promotions company in the world, Dana managed high profile fighters such as Chuck Liddell, which provided him with early awareness of small but powerful MMA organizations such as a new start-up MMA event called the Ultimate Fighting Championship. In 2001, when Dana was made aware of the fact that the business owners who were running the UFC wanted to sell the company for a mere $2,000,000, Dana engaged Frank and Lorenzo Fertitta, two men who had previously made their fortunes in the Nevada casino business, and persuaded them to purchase the UFC. The purchase was made and Dana was promoted to the position of President for the newly reformed UFC. From 2001 onward, Dana White and the Fertittas have not only taken the UFC from a money-losing enterprise to becoming a company estimated to be worth several billions of dollars, they also were a critical part of the major growth and awareness of the sport. Dana's vision is to make MMA and the UFC as large, if not larger than, organizations such as football's National Football League (NFL), and looking at what he's been able to accomplish within the scope of ten short years, he'll probably do just that.

If you've not ever seen Dana White in action, you can go to Youtube.com and view past pre—and post-fight press events, as well as his interviews with various media entities. One of the characteristics and qualities of Dana White that you'll quickly identify is that he pretty much says what is on his mind. There's not a lot of sugar-coating answers or dodging questions with him.

Dana exhibits the type of executive candor that some might find a bit brash, and he releases "f-bombs" like they are grammatically required to complete a sentence. This candor and straightforward approach to communication works, and in the case of developing the UFC into the powerhouse that it is today, the proof of his effectiveness is obvious. In describing Dana White, Ultimate MMA magazine wrote, "outspoken, driven and charismatic, Dana White lives and breathes fighting." If more CEOs worked as hard and as focused as Dana White does, America would regain our global dominance in the market place in record time.

Another example of effective leadership in MMA can be found with Scott Coker, the founder and CEO for Strikeforce, an MMA organization that promotes fights with high profile fighters such as Tyron Woodley, and Tim Kennedy. In recent years, the sport of mixed martial arts has seen promotion companies come and go, but Strikeforce has remained strong and continues to grow and gain fans with each fight it offers. Scott has a foundational connection to MMA in the form of the fifth degree black belt that he holds in Taekwondo.

Up until March of 2011, Strikeforce and the UFC, as natural competitors, were in constant battle with each other while working to grow two organizations competing in an extremely dynamic marketplace. That changed in 2011 when Zuffa LLC, the parent company of the UFC, purchased the Strikeforce organization.

While both companies will operate as separate entities, the acquisition will now allow both organizations to capitalize on economies of scale, and best practices, as well as share a parent company that is now the undisputed leader in the MMA promotion marketplace. Scott Coker is a dynamic leader and CEOs of other industries should look at Coker as a reference point on how to stay competitive and work to grow a business in an aggressive, young industry.

Across the globe, there are hundreds of smaller promoters and organizations that are working to host local market MMA events that are helping to promote the sport, as well as provide a forum for up and coming fighters to develop their skills and improve their fighting records. In my home state of Indiana alone, local event promoters such as Legends of Fighting and Colosseum Combat are hosting incredible fights that are expanding the MMA fan base. These organizations are also providing an excellent opportunity for some dynamic Hoosier fighters to gain experience and develop their career in MMA. Another Indiana operation that is working to expand the MMA fan base on a national level is cagecraze.com.

Cagecraze.com is an MMA social network that provides MMA updates, news, and options for fans and fighters to interact on topics ranging from favorite fighter discussions to understanding state regulations for unarmed combat competitions. These are solid examples of local leadership and the level of entrepreneurial drive needed to expand the awareness of the sport and grow it to the next level of success.

This is why effective leadership is important. If you don't have it, taking an organization, a sport, or even a country to the next level of progress is next to impossible or at the very least, an extreme uphill battle.

Also, it is important to understand that there is a difference between being a leader and being a manager. While a great leader will know how to manage, and a great manager will know how to be a leader, the primary difference between both positions is that a leader builds, defines, and sets the momentum that defines a corporation or organization. A manager is normally an individual who takes what has been established and ensures people follow the defined path and achieve goals and objectives. Peter Drucker, the famous writer and management consultant, once said that the difference between a manager and a leader is "management is doing things right; leadership is doing the right things."(35)

The world of business has offered us example after example of leaders who built incredible companies from scratch, but once the business got to a certain point of success, managers were hired in order to ensure the day-to-day business was monitored, supervised, and specific processes and procedures were followed.

This is important to realize because if you become a manager and find yourself thinking that you should be the one leading the company and defining its future direction and course, this is a natural progression of leadership and you should embrace this additional yearning for leadership that you possess.

Some people in management generate incredible success in their role, but don't want anything to do with creating something from scratch or being the person that sets the future course for a company or organization. Again, this discovery is normal and it's better to understand your desires and expectations rather than moving into a role that might make you unhappy in the process.

Regardless if you become the President of the UFC or work to manage a group of Boy Scouts, leadership and management are critical to all aspects of life, and people who are good at running events, organizations, and companies are always needed.

THE PERKS OF LEADERSHIP

With effective leadership comes the opportunity for perks and benefits that range from monetary gains, additional freedom, and access to events, people, and rewards to which others either cannot gain access, or have to pay substantial fees in order to attend. Leadership can be difficult and without benefits of assuming the position of leadership, most would more than likely be happy with just staying out of the line of fire. There are logical reasons why people put themselves in the position of leadership other than the obvious answer of gaining power.

For some, leadership is just a way of life and being on point is simply how some desire to operate. World famous Muay Thai instructor Marc Dellagrotte once said, "I am just the type of guy that if I can't steer the ship, if I can't be the captain, I would prefer not to be onboard."(36)

Some of the best benefits I have gained from being in a position of leadership are actually being able to help others grow, and making a difference in other people's lives. I believe that by serving others, a leader actually gains more personally.

A leader that is only focused on their own personal gain might rise to a certain level of leadership, but they normally do not last very long and the people working for them will more than likely cherish the day this individual falls, and most end up doing just that.

Other than the potential for higher pay and access to other perks, additional benefits of being in a position of leadership include:

- Watching yourself grow as an individual when you address good and bad times within the organization that you're supporting
- Being a mentor to people who are looking to move into leadership
- Watching your ideas and visions become a reality, as well as watching others follow your plans and support your ideas
- Better understanding your strengths and areas of improvement
- Setting the course and direction for a group of people, organization, or effort
- Positioning yourself for even greater personal and professional gains
- Assisting your greater community and/or endeavors that you're working to see grow
- Making a difference in your life, the lives of others, and the interests and people that you serve and support

THE PRICE OF LEADERSHIP

The famous American writer John Updike once said that "A leader is one who, out of madness or goodness, volunteers to take upon himself the woe of the people. There are few men so foolish, hence the erratic quality of leadership in the world."(37) Being a leader isn't always about smiles and good times. Leadership can be difficult, and can expose the leader to situations that will test the hell of them over and over again. Personally, I've had to experience situations such as having to tell a group of 70 people working for me that their jobs were being eliminated and outsourced to another country. For me, this experience was very difficult because it impacted people that I cared about, as well as people who had generated solid results, but simply fell victim to changing business conditions that focused on reducing overhead costs. My message to the team had always been that if we worked hard, generated results, and put clients first, good things would happen, and yet this was not the case.

From a lesson in leadership perspective, this situation was one hell of an eye opener for me, but I would have rather learned this lesson by reading a book or a business case rather than experience it firsthand. If you're going to assume the position of leadership, sometimes you don't have the luxury of dictating what experiences or lessons you'll learn; you just have to work with what happens the best you can.

Another lesson in leadership that I learned early in my career was **YOU are responsible.**

While this might sound like the most basic of lessons in leadership, it's actually a fact that many people in the role of leadership do not understand. I learned how responsible a leader is when I joined the United States Navy and while in boot camp, I decided to volunteer to be a leader in our squadron. I was responsible for a group of young men within my squadron, and this meant that I was on point for ensuring they knew how to do everything from folding laundry to working their assigned duties. If you've not ever served in the Navy, one of the skills that you are taught in boot camp is how to fold your clothing in a manner that will allow you to pack a complete sea bag of clothes, and still have room for personal items and toiletries. The joke in the Navy was that by the time a sailor graduated from boot camp, he would be able to fold his underwear into the size of a quarter. One day, our company commander was doing his daily inspection of our squad and he stopped by the locker of a young man on my team.

This individual had totally jacked up how he had folded his t-shirts and the next thing I know, the company commander was yelling my name. "Johnson, get your [expletive] over here!" is the scream I heard across the barracks. I ran over to the company commander and he proceeded to get in my face, yelling, "Did you show this idiot how to fold his underwear?" Unfortunately, I replied, "Yeah, I showed him how to fold his underwear." For those of you who have not been in the service, you don't answer officers or company commanders with anything other than a "yes, sir" or "No, sir." You simply don't say, "Yeah, I showed him how to fold his underwear."

The next thing I remember, my company commander is in my face yelling some very colorful and character-building sentences, but out of all the things he yelled, I was particularly shocked to hear one sentence, which was, "You're going to I.T.!"

I.T. stood for intensive training, which meant that in addition to the exercises and work that I had to complete that day, at night when everyone else was relaxing and writing home, I would be sent to the gym where a group of what I could only classify as "Death Nazis" worked me and a group of other degenerates into a nice sweat. We had to run, do push-ups, sit-ups, flutter-kicks, pull-up's, and you name it, for a full two hours. When I got back to the barracks, I saw the guy in my group who hadn't properly folded his t-shirt that day, and he was in our break room drinking a coke and laughing with his friends. Two thoughts immediately came to my mind. The first one was could I kill this kid and get away with it, and the second was why the hell did I volunteer to be a squad leader in the first place?

Then a funny thing happened the next day. I got with all of the guys in my group and made sure their dumb asses knew how to fold their clothes and then I inspected their lockers myself. I did not want another butt-chewing by my company commander and I sure as hell did not want to go back to intensive training. Lesson heard and clearly understood, sir. If you're in a position of leadership and your people jack stuff up, YOU'RE responsible and need to get it addressed and fixed.

Another price of leadership that some will pay is the mismanagement of power. Power itself can be a perk of leadership for those who have a desire to gain it, but power can also be a dangerous side benefit of leadership. For some, power is their downfall and their gain of power goes straight to their heads. I'm of the school of thought that the abuse of power is generated by two separate root causes. The first root cause is lack of confidence and leadership skills. The act of gaining power is not what spirals some out of control; it's the fact that they don't know how to effectively lead without showing they are clearly and dominantly in control. If someone questions their authority, this person will be dealt with severely because the leader does not know how to function when their actions or words are called into question. So in reality, this person is not necessarily power hungry as much as they are lacking confidence or the skills required to work with people who might posture against them. An effective leader knows that one of the best ways to defuse an individual who postures against you, is to be confident and work to listen to an individual rather than shut down and blast this person for their incorrect actions.

The second root cause is in fact the individual that is power hungry and has assumed the position of leadership simply for the ability to control and take advantage of other people. It is an unfortunate truth that there are people in management and overall leadership that fall into this category. We've all known someone like this, and unfortunately, many of us have worked with people like this.

One of the really bad things about challenging economic times and periods of high unemployment is the fact that this is a perfect time for really bad leaders to make life hell for the people working for them. Bad leaders know that people are concerned about the economy and the job market, so the leaders are allowed to get away with treating people like dirt. Please remember two things:

1.) What comes around goes around, and the universe has a unique way of delivering good things to good people and ensuring bad/negative people get what they deserve.
2.) Many times bad leaders are just hiding insecurities and fear of failure. The challenge is more than likely not you; it's them.

If you're working for a manager or leader like that now, I feel for you, but my experience has shown me a couple of things over the years. First, bad leaders don't stick around for very long. It seems like you're going to work for them forever, but I think you'll be surprised how they quickly move out of your life.

Second, learn from these people. In life you're going to work with and for people who will show you the right way to manage business and how to work with people. During times that you're working with people who are less effective, watch what they are doing wrong and don't ever duplicate it! In life, a negative situation can be just as effective (sometimes more effective) of a lesson than a positive one. In the past when I worked with less than effective managers, I took copious notes on what they did wrong and made a clear plan of how I would never manage people. People will walk through fire for people who take care of them and work to protect their interests and concerns.

People will throw bad managers into the fire at their first possible chance. Always take care of your people and build a team focused on success and results. Remember, in all aspects of life, the person that is focused on taking care of other people and serving others is best off in the long run. Mohammed Ali, one of history's greatest boxers, once said, "Service to others is the rent you pay for your room here on earth,"(53) and these are good words to live by.

Unfortunately, the world of MMA is not void of ineffective or corrupt leadership. There are countless examples of promoters who have gone out of business due to unscrupulous business practices that range from not complying with local gaming commission sanctioning rules, to not paying professional fighters after bouts.

The sad truth is that some people are simply after a quick buck regardless of the havoc they create or the wrong they do in the process. The good news is there are people such as yourself who want to lead and serve others. The greater number of results-oriented leaders that are in a position to support sports such as MMA, the bigger, better, and more beneficial the sport will be to the people who work within it, as well as the fans who watch and enjoy it. There is a price to be paid not only from the individual who accepts the position of leadership, but for the lack of effective leadership in general. This is why it is critical for those who want to lead to do so with the intentions of being the best that they can be, and to also honestly and effectively serve the organization, people, or cause for which they have decided to serve in a leadership capacity.

With good intentions and solid leadership skills acting as the wind that stabilizes your sails of success and progress in life, you'll find that the price you pay in order to be a leader, no matter how many times you might have to go to boot camp's intensive training, will be worth it in the end. There is no greater reward than knowing that the direction and course you set to follow generated success for yourself, and the people under your guidance, and that the organization or effort you're leading is growing and prospering because of your leadership.

HOW TO DEVELOP YOUR LEADERSHIP SKILLS

Regardless if it's mastering a discipline within mixed martial arts or working to gain leadership experience, the best way to enhance your skills is to actually get involved, gain experience, and get your hands dirty. Before I started taking MMA classes, I understood the basics of Brazilian Jiu Jitsu submissions, but after taking classes and actually performing the submissions (and getting caught in them) I learned a hell of a lot more about the techniques than I did by simply watching them on television. With that said, if you're looking to expand and enhance your skills in leadership, you put yourself in the position of leadership as much as you possibly can. If you're a student and not working within a management position just yet, you can gain valuable leadership skills by volunteering with community organizations that are looking for people to help with design and managed projects.

Perhaps you belong to a church that supports local mission work, or maybe where you live has a neighborhood association that you can run or assume a supporting leadership role to help out and gain experience. The point is, if you wait for leadership experience and positions to come to you, you might lose valuable time and exposure that would help you maximize and optimize your skills. Political and spiritual leader, Mahatma Gandhi, once said that "The history of the world is full of men who rose to leadership, by sheer force of self-confidence, bravery and tenacity."(38) In addition to working to begin gaining leadership and management experience, you can do the following to prepare for future leadership success:

- **Find a mentor**: One of the best ways to learn how to effectively do something is to find someone who is currently doing well and mirror their techniques and solutions. Remember the old saying "find someone who has what you want, do what they do, and you'll get what they got." It's not the most grammatically correct saying you'll ever hear, but it makes a lot of sense and it works.

- **Study current leaders who are generating results**: Regardless of your area of focus, be it business, politics, academics, or life in general, if you want to start learning what effective leaders do and don't do, study up on today's industry leaders. If you're looking to build an empire from scratch, who better to study than individuals like Bill Gates. If you want to mirror effective wealth building leadership, you can research Warren Buffet. The list is endless and the pool is deep with solid leaders to learn from, as well as examples of leaders from which you'll learn what not to do in a given field of interest.

You can read magazines, books, listen to podcasts, and watch televised interviews and updates. Gaining information and accessing facts about today's effective leaders is easier to do now than at any time in history. Use data and examples of solid and successful leadership to jump start your personal development.

- **Take a class:** There's an old Chinese proverb that states that "Learning is a treasure that will follow its owner everywhere." Today, the opportunities to gain an education or further develop one's existing education are greater than at any time in history. In addition to traditional universities, organizations such as Dale Carnegie offer excellent courses on topics ranging from sales to management. By taking courses or even obtaining a degree in a given subject, you will gain a competitive edge. Personally, I believe that on-the-job experience is just as important as academic exposure to a subject, and the individual who gains both formal knowledge and actual job experience will have an advantage for generating success and results. Even if it's taking an online course, get access to training today.

- **Start planning now:** Rather than waiting to gain a position of leadership before you start to plan how you will generate results, start planning today. Obviously, your plans will have to be tweaked once you're actually in the role of leadership, but at least your mind is on the course of defining what you want to accomplish and what results you're looking to achieve. Act as if you were in the role today and start to think about situations that you might experience and how you would handle them. The utilization of mental imagery is extremely powerful.

The more you use your mind to run through scenarios such as handling negotiations, working escalations, and presenting in front of clients and your employees, the more prepared you will be when you complete these functions in reality. The mind is a powerful tool that will allow you to run through scenarios in a manner that will allow you to work out solutions, establish initial plans, and gain an awareness of your strengths and weaknesses. When you act as if you are already in a position of leadership, be it a specific position or leadership in general, your mind will start to work in the manner that will allow you to plan and prepare for situations. Obviously, as you gain the position in reality, you'll encounter things that you did not plan for and some of the things that you did plan for will be different than what you initially imagined, but at least your mind is prepared for the position and you'll only have to tweak your plan rather than gain experience and set plans from scratch. Your mind is your most powerful muscle, so use it to your advantage and allow it to help you generate success.

- **Start a business:** One of the most effective ways that I believe people can gain solid leadership skills is by starting their own business. I've started several businesses on the side throughout the years and it was an incredible way for me to learn and develop critical skills such as selling, marketing, planning, accounting, negotiating, and customer service. Early in my career I wanted to move up the proverbial corporate ladder, but I lacked experience and vernacular to talk about business conditions and required criteria to run elements of a business.

By starting my own company I picked up skills that it would have taken me years to develop in my corporate position, and the business also generated additional funds for myself and my family. I ran these businesses on the side while I worked full-time, and there was even a time when I worked a full-time job, had a part-time business, and went to college. Sure I was busy, but I'm the kind of person that likes to stay busy and feel that I'm using my time to develop as a business and prepare for the next level of success in life. Even if you start a basic s-corporation and work something on the side for five to fifteen hours a week, you'll be gaining some incredible experience, as well as, a better understanding of your areas of strength and areas you need to improve in relative to business. It's not hard to start a company so just think about something you'd like to do on the side and get started today. Who knows, it might be the next Microsoft that you're starting, but even if it's a mega-small business that only generates $1, you'll learn a lot.

T.K.O. (Tips, Knowledge, and Objectives)

There are several advanced applications, techniques, and solutions to further develop the power of your mind. One such program is Neuro-Linguistics Programming or NLP. NLP was created by John Grinder and Richard Bandler, and it's a proven way for people to train their mind to re-program mind associations to generate new results and ultimately additional success in life. To learn more about NLP, go to www.NLP.com.

TRAITS OF AN EFFECTIVE LEADER

While every effective leader is different and might utilize unique methods and solutions to lead people and generate results, there are similarities that can be found in successful leadership. During your life you'll work with multiple leaders and you'll start to see how the successful ones master and deploy a common set of techniques that generate results. You'll also more than likely work for some leaders who totally fail, and even in this situation you'll see that the reason for their failure was because they did not master and/or deploy one or more of the areas of focus below.

- **Listen:** One of the most powerful traits of a successful leader is the ability to just shut up and listen. So many people in the position of leadership are constantly asked to talk about their opinions, talk about the direction of the company, talk about yada, yada, yada. While it's important for a leader to speak (see below), it's critical for a leader to listen. When employees and customers feel that they are being heard, it makes a difference and can directly impact areas of critical importance such as morale, sales, customer satisfaction, and it also allows the leader to learn. There is a reason why God gave us two ears and only one mouth. Listen more and speak less.
- **Speak:** As mentioned above, a leader should focus on listening as much as possible, but when it is time to speak, their words should be powerful. History is rich with examples of leaders who have used the power of the spoken word to motivate, lead, and change the world.

Leaders such as Dr. Martin Luther King Jr. and Ronald Reagan are just two examples of men galvanized in our history books for not only their results, but the incredible power of their ability to speak. In the world of MMA, Dana White is an excellent example of an effective speaker. As previously mentioned, Dana is quite outspoken, and I would not say that he possesses an eloquent tongue that comes close to the likes of a Ronald Reagan or Dr. Martin Luther King Jr., but when Dana speaks, people listen and by the time he's done they clearly know where he stands on a given topic. Sure he'll drop a couple dozen "f-bombs" on reporters asking him to comment on heated topics, but his message is always clear and he is incredibly candid during his discussions. Even with his high degree of candor, he is fair with allowing people to speak and share their questions and opinions. When it is time for you to speak, be clear and concise with your message because your people are listening to you.

T.K.O. (Tips, Knowledge, and Objectives)

The fear of public speaking has been identified as a fear that ranks above heights and financial failure. Most people feel a degree of nervousness and anxiety before speaking to a group of people, but this fear becomes greatly reduced with experience and confidence. Toastmasters International is an excellent organization that works with individuals to improve their speaking skills, as well as provide a safe forum to gain experience and confidence while speaking. To learn more about Toastmasters in your area, visit www.toastmasters.org.

- **Establish a vision:** If a leader does not create and share his or her vision on where they want to take a company or organization, people will follow aimlessly, or in some cases won't follow at all. A vision statement needs to be clear, achievable stretch goal. A stretch goal is a goal that means an individual or organization needs to really work hard to achieve an objective, but the objective is achievable. When I was the leader of a team of 80 Customer Service Representatives that managed and processed over one billion dollars in annual business, the vision statement that I created for the team was: ***To be the most effective order management and client satisfaction solution . . . period!***
  - ***We deliver effective communication.***
  - ***We are responsive.***
  - ***We understand that our input and contributions count.***
  - ***We deliver outrageous client satisfaction.***
  - ***We take pride in our work.***

This team later went on to be recognized as the first group to win a company-wide contest for excellence in client satisfaction. When I created the vision statement, I wanted the team to know that I expected them to be the best within our company and I stressed the areas in which I wanted us to excel. In order to reach a destination a team needs to understand where they are going and what is expected from them. Vision statements accomplish this objective and allow a leader to set the direction and expectations of a team, organization, or company.

- **Motivate your people:** Leaders who know how to motivate their people get results. Effective leaders know that people are motivated in different ways. Some people are driven solely by monetary rewards (i.e. paycheck, bonuses, etc.); others are motivated by status, rank, and promotion within an organization; and others simply want the occasional pat on the back to stay happy. Effective leaders know the best way to understand what motivates their employees is simply to ask them. People will tell you what keeps them engaged and willing to work hard. The people in positions of power who are not concerned about motivating their workforce might generate results, but nowhere near the level that they would if they had a team that was fired up and willing to give blood, sweat, and tears towards a cause. Find out what motivates your people and ensure they are rewarded in the way they want to be rewarded.

- **Understand the industry and market conditions:** Dynamic leaders know that they have to understand their industry and know the conditions and factors impacting their industry and business. The reason why this element of leadership is so important is twofold. First, the people on your team look to you to provide guidance, feedback, and direction as to what is ahead of the company and what must be done to take them to the next level of success. If your answer is "The heck if I know." when your people ask you about the business forecast, you will lose credibility fast. Monitor your business and consult with analysts in your industry, or at least read publications to keep track of your market.

Also, collect and use data within your business to track and report on productivity, profit and loss analysis, sales figures, and customer satisfaction ratings. The more you can educate and inform your team members, the more they will feel involved and engaged in the business. The more engaged and informed your team is, the more they will work to build the business.

- **Put people first:** A weak leader (and a person who doesn't even deserve to be in a position of leadership) fails to put their employees first. People will walk through fire for leaders who they know have their back and best interests in mind. Equally true, leaders who only put the business and their personal interests into consideration will eventually get thrown into the fire. In other words, if a person in a leadership position does not take care of his or her people, they might have people who will work for them, but there is zero loyalty and the employees are just waiting for the opportunity to get this person fired. Be a leader who is passionate about your people and put them first. Greg Jackson, one of the most recognized coaches within the MMA industry, is an example of a leader that puts people first. For the professional fighters Jackson trains, he does not charge them money and only accepts money if the fighter wants to pay him.

The law of reciprocity states that what you give back to the universe is returned to you. If you offer good and do good, then an even greater degree of good is returned back to you. I believe that taking care of people and doing good by people is an excellent way for you to achieve success.

What you give will be returned to you in spades. People will know that you are working hard for them and they will reciprocate the loyalty and effort, and generate incredible results for you. Be a leader focused on ensuring your people are well taken care of.

- **Get to know the customer:** A situation that I see happen often is the farther up the corporate ladder some leaders get, the farther away they get from their customers. The very component of their business (the customer) becomes less known to them, and yet they make business decisions that will ultimately impact the client. Also, the more layers of management between the client and the leader, the less the leader will know anything about the customer and challenges of their business that are impacting the client. No one wants their boss to know about problems and thus by the time challenges reach the top, the situation is filtered, watered down, and minimized to maybe a brief reporting fact. What this means for the leader who does not actively work to stay engaged with clients is that the leader quickly gets into a position where they really don't know anything about the clients. Then the leader will eventually talk with a client or talk with employees about customer desires and people will be thinking "What the heck are you talking about?" It's not a good place to be but it happens every day in organizations all across the globe. As an effective leader, stay close to your customers. Listen to them. Ask them questions and then shut the hell up when they answer you.

Customers are your life blood and if you're running your operation without knowing the DNA of your clients, it's a guarantee you're bound for challenges. Be an effective leader and stay in front of your clients no matter what position you obtain within your organization.

- **Be passionate:** Passion is the power that fuels every success story. Passion is the energy that drives people to start businesses, win championships, and excel in life. Passion is what maintains motivation during the hard times and amplifies the joy when victory is achieved. An endeavor pursued but not fueled by passion might be successful, but also might be less fruitful. To be passionate about something and to achieve success in your area of passion is the ultimate goal of achievement.

If you ever want to see an example of passion in action in the world of mixed martial arts, just tune in to an event with fighters such as Clay Guida or Diego Sanchez. Both of these guys are crazy, out of their minds, passionate about what they do and it's obvious. To become the best (and enjoy what you're doing) at anything, you have to have passion. A leader who is passionate about what he or she is doing creates an attitude that becomes infectious among employees. If your people just see you going through the motions, they will do the same. If your people see you jacked out of your mind excited and passionate about growing the business and helping them grow, they will join in line with this passion. Everyone wants to be motivated and passionate about what they're doing in life, and no one wants to live a life of complacency and dullness.

Live your life with passion and make people become passionate just by simply being around you and getting caught in the energy that surrounds you while you live out the life that you've planned for yourself.

RULES OF THE OCTAGON

Rule #6: Become an effective leader

Remember, if you're not leading, you're following. If you're a natural follower, then this statement might be acceptable to you, but remember, people who don't lead, or choose to follow ineffective leaders, can't complain about the direction that things take in their work and in their lives. Only when you lead can you feel in control of the direction and decisions impacting your life. Now with that said, a trait of an effective leader is the ability to follow the lead of other equally or higher qualified leaders (i.e. Division Vice-President follows the direction of the Chief Executive Officer), but even when following, a leader will ensure they are involved in the process and that their presence is felt. Take control of the reins and generate success, generate results, and generate the level of accomplishment that you're destined to create. Also, understand while mastering the skills of being a great leader, one must realize the following truths of leadership:

- **Successful leaders learn from failure:** Even the best mixed martial artists can lose fights. Chances are that, you will experience some form of delay, set back, or failure in life.

Our focus should always be on the positive and always expecting to win, but if you do experience a challenge, be it in a job, a lost sale, a relationship, a test, whatever the case may be, remember that successful leaders will learn from the failure. Within the experience of the loss, you will gain valuable insight about yourself, as well as clear direction on how to avoid the failure in the future. Learn from your mistakes and understand that even the best can experience challenges. Just learn to overcome them and never repeat the same mistake twice.

- **Sometimes no matter what you do, the stuff is going to hit the fan:** Successful leaders understand that sometimes bad things can happen no matter what you've done to prepare for success. It's just part of life. As a manager, you might receive a corporate directive that calls for outsourcing your team to another country (and I've had this happen). You might have to lay off hard working people who have families that need their income to survive. You might have to skip awarding bonuses because of outside economic factors. The list goes on regarding situations you have little control over, yet will substantially impact you and your people. When situations like this happen, successful leaders work to minimize the impact as much as possible, work to ensure those not impacted remain as motivated as possible, and work to do what is possible to prevent the situation from happening again. Remember, a true leader shows his or her worth during the challenging times, not the good times. Anyone can lead during the good times, but only real leaders know how to lead when times get tough.

- **Leaders are not always popular:** If you've decided to become a leader because you want to be popular, chances are that you will be in for a surprise. Even people-focused leaders have to make decisions that are not always popular. Perhaps it's an announcement that mandatory overtime is required, or maybe it's the feedback that you have to provide to an employee who is not pulling their weight (who will be angry at you even though they are the one causing the challenge). Leaders can be respected and liked, but if you lead with the sole purpose of being liked and being popular, you're more than likely going to fail. Work to serve your people and work to generate results. Making tough calls and sometimes unpopular decisions is part of the role, so be prepared to do what is required and learn to develop thick skin in the process.

- **Effective leadership can make a difference:** This is the best part of being a leader. You can make a difference in not only the role, but more important, with the people that follow you. Even the small things count. For a long time, I saved a note that one of my employees gave me one day. I was able to get her a raise that she had been requesting for some time. Times were tight but I went to battle for her and was able to secure a higher wage increase than what she requested. It made her feel great, but it made me feel even better. Another time, when I assumed leadership of another team, I had an employee come to me and mention that she had an overtime error on her paycheck and she never received $200 that was owed to her. I contacted payroll and was told that they could not go back and make the adjustment.

Rather than dealing with the rhetoric of working with payroll, I just nominated the employee to receive a bonus of $200, so not only did she get her money, it came to her in the form of a bonus reward. Something that she had been working to resolve for months before I arrived was resolved in less than two weeks. I was able to make a difference and also show my team that if they worked to generate results, I would be working for them to generate results.

The world needs leaders and effective leadership. We have example after example these days of ineffective, dishonest, and disloyal leaders who are only focused on themselves and the bottom line. While the bottom line is important, I challenge you to become a people-focused leader and be the driver of decisions and results. Make a difference in your life, and equally important, make a difference in the lives of others and the efforts/organizations that you support in a leadership capacity.

THE SCORECARD

- *UNDERSTAND THAT IF YOU'RE NOT LEADING, YOU'RE FOLLOWING*
- *BE A PEOPLE-FOCUSED LEADER*
- *LEADERSHIP WILL HIGHLIGHT YOUR SKILLS, AS WELL AS REQUIRED AREAS OF IMPROVEMENT*
- *AS A LEADER YOU ARE RESPONSIBLE*
- *EFFECTIVE LEADERSHIP MAKES A DIFFERENCE IN ORGANIZATIONS AND WITH PEOPLE*

Dealing with setback and failure

"At some point, I'm going to lose. GSP is going to lose. Anderson Silva is going to lose. Maybe it won't be fighting, but at something else in life. A true champion shows they can come back from that adversity." Josh Koscheck(39)

THE REALITY OF LOSS

The most important rule to remember when it comes to losing is . . . never lose! Now with that said, it is an unfortunate truth for the majority of us in life, be it a relationship, a business deal, or even in competitive combat, that we are all going to experience a loss in one shape or another. Even the pound-for-pound best fighters in mixed martial arts such as Georges St. Pierre, Jose Aldo, and Anderson Silva all have losses on their fight records. Think about it, not only have fighting legends like Georges St. Pierre and Anderson Silva lost once, they both have multiple losses on their fight records.

The chance of experiencing a loss or a setback in life is a reality. This might not sound like a topic you expect to see in a book focused on building success-oriented attitudes and generating results based on winner mentalities, but to not discuss the topic of losing would rob you of a valuable lesson in life.

In fact, losing can be an even more life changing educational experience than what some wins will provide to you in your life.

Anthony Robbins, author of *Awaken the Giants* and an international expert on the topic of success and motivation, once said that, "I've come to believe that all of my past failure and frustration were actually laying the foundation for the understandings that have created the new level of living I now enjoy."(40) I'm definitely not saying that you should get in the habit of losing in order to grow in life, but realize that if you do experience a loss, there is a way to capitalize on the situation.

CAPITALIZING FROM A LOSS

The first way to capitalize from setback is to **learn from the setback**. Henry Ford once said that, "Failure is simply the opportunity to begin again, this time more intelligently."(41) If you experience a setback and you don't take the time to analyze what you might have done wrong, then you're likely to make the same mistake twice. Setback comes to us either because the timing wasn't right or we weren't fully prepared to achieve success. When you experience a setback, take the time to review what occurred and what you will do going forward to prevent the loss from happening again. Regardless, of your profession or position in life, it's critical that you analyze what worked for you during a situation and what was the root cause of your failure.

With that in mind, here's a word of caution for you. Be careful of your initial analysis especially if the loss was painful or meant a lot to you. The reason why I say this is because emotions can get the best of us and the first thing that we think of to define the root cause of the challenge might not be the real problem. One of the things that I've learned while working with MMA fighters is that right after a loss in the cage I am prepared to hear some crazy excuses. I've heard things such as, "I gassed out because I have a cold," or "The stupid referee was not watching the fight," and I even saw one fighter totally rip his corner man a new rear after a loss because he felt that when the corner man told him that he needed to do something spectacular in the final round, it threw him off course. I was next to the corner man when he told the fighter that the fight was really close and he needed to really pour it on in the final round. This is something that most corners will do and yet it was the reason this fighter lost. Losing hurts and it's a natural instinct to try to externalize the reason for the loss, so realize what you pinpoint as an initial issue might actually not be the challenge once you've had some time to calm down and think about the situation more clearly. There might just be an external reason for the loss; just ensure you're not blaming something that might not have anything to do with the situation.

The reason why this is important is because if you're focusing on correcting the wrong thing, chances are that you will repeat the same error because your root cause was incorrect all along. Learn from your losses and make them build you into an even more effective and unstoppable individual.

The second way to capitalize from setback is to understand that **everything happens for a reason**. Some things will happen in your life that will really test this school of thought, but for me, the statement has rung true over and over. For example, I once worked for this marketing company that established merchant credit card accounts for small to medium-sized businesses in the state of Indiana. The opportunity sounded like an incredible way to make loads of cash while offering a service that practically every business needed, and the position even offered daily leads that were supposedly ripe for the closing. I started working for the organization and I quickly found out that the leads weren't as "ripe" as I had hoped. For some reason the company had me traveling literally hundreds of miles a day to small towns and to companies that didn't even have clients asking to use their credit cards when purchasing product. I even had some business owners tell me that they only agreed to meet me just to get off the phone with the pushy telemarketer who was setting up the leads for me. I also found out that the monthly lease that I was asking the clients to pay was way higher than competitors, and our average merchant discount rates were also higher than the norm. So with a couple thousand miles on my car and only a couple of dollars made in my pocket, I became discouraged.

Actually, I became pissed off. I just wanted to offer a good product and service to my clients and pay my bills. Then fate stepped in. I found out that there were other merchant companies in different states and so I reached out to a few firms close to Indiana.

I learned that I could process my own applications and avoid having to work with the company that was charging the higher fees in Indiana. My cost to process an application was only $150 and I could charge a considerably smaller amount per month off the equipment. With this new knowledge in hand, I started a merchant processing business and focused on clients close to my home office. I placed an ad in the Yellow Pages and business was literally coming to me. My rates were very competitive and I closed tons of business. I then struck up a deal with a couple of local banks to support clients that they could not approve and I only had to pay the referring representatives $50 per lead that I closed. I was averaging $500 a deal for business that was basically coming to me locally. I then started processing merchant accounts nationally and I turned a part-time business that I created on the side into an easy to manage business that was generating an additional $25,000 a year for me. So what started out as a bad situation for me actually became a very good situation. If I wouldn't have worked for that marketing company I never would have learned the ins and outs of the merchant business which made the start up of my own business flow as easy as it did.

Everything happens for a reason; you just have to look for the reason. Sometimes the reason is immediate and sometimes it takes years to find out why things happen. If you experience a setback or loss, take the time to review the situation and look for the lesson learned in your experience. Start to realize that good will come from a situation you initially view as a negative. It may take time, but the good will appear.

The third way to capitalize from setback is to **use the loss as motivation**. The old saying goes that "Hell hath no fury like a woman scorned" but I believe there should also be a saying that states, "Hell's fury ain't jack compared to a man or a woman motivated by loss." Experiencing a setback will either break a person or make them rock hard. Olympic track super star Wilma Rudolph once said, "Winning is great, sure, but if you are really going to do something in life, the secret is learning how to lose. Nobody goes undefeated all the time. If you can pick up after a crushing defeat, and go on to win again, you are going to be a champion someday."(42) Many believe that a fighter is never the same after they experience a loss, but I believe the difference is either a good change or a bad change depending on how the person allowed the loss to impact them. If a fighter was knocked out during his last fight, then he might go into the next bout worried that his chin is weak now and perhaps his chances of getting knocked out again are good. With this fear in his mind, he is hesitant in the cage, covering up, moving back, and then just as he feared, the punch comes and he hits the canvas.

The fighter motivated by his setback will understand that he is human, that if he does not expand and improve on the things that caused him to lose his last fight, he will experience the same pain again. But unlike the fighter who gets knocked out again because of the fear of loss, the motivated fighter will harness the energy and the frustration of losing and use this as fuel to train harder, to improve techniques, endurance, speed, power, and agility.

They will use the energy of the loss to grow their hunger for success. How many successful businesses have been spawned by men or women who were driven with passion fueled by wanting to show an ex-spouse that they will be great without them? These are the kind of people that, when pushed down, come back up even harder, better, and with more intensity. Use any setback that you experience to fuel your passion to want to come back with a vengeance, to show people that you get back up when you're knocked down, and that you realize losing is just a sign that you need to improve in an area of life but once mastered, you'll be even better than before.

T.K.O. (Tips, Knowledge, and Objectives)

There are times when losing makes complete sense. During negotiation training, people are taught that some deals are not worth winning and one should look at the alternatives of not making a deal, as well as the costs of making said deal. If you win a negotiation and close a deal that actually loses you money, then ultimately you lost. If you consciously decide to lose one component of a negotiation to win a much larger component, then you win. Always review your situations to ensure what you're winning is worth it and also know that some of your losses are a true blessing in disguise.

BUILDING CONFIDENCE FROM LOSS

The great motivator Napoleon Hill once said, "Every adversity, every failure, every heartache carries with it the seed of an equal or greater benefit."(43) Now if you tell that to someone right after they got tapped out (submitted) or knocked out in an MMA bout, you're likely to hear some colorful expletives, if not get knocked out yourself. After the emotions calm down and the person is allowed to evaluate the situation, they eventually will see that what Mr. Hill says above is true. Remember, at the end of the day, you don't want to lose or experience setback, but if you do, realize that experience will be gained and even benefits can be realized from the situation. One of the things that you will notice that you gain from the loss is a new appreciation for victory. Malcolm Forbes, Publisher of *Forbes* magazine, once said that "Victory is sweetest when you've known defeat."(44) Just like the old saying goes, you don't know what you've lost until it's gone, and regaining what you lost will take on a new passion and re-ignite the fire inside your soul to gain back what is rightfully yours. So while losing is not something we want to do, if you do experience a setback, use the experience to light the proverbial fire under your butt; use it to remind yourself what it was that you had and want back; and use it to really appreciate those things previously lost once you've earned them back. Be it money, recognition, status, a relationship, whatever, just appreciate what it is that you earn back.

Another thing that can be gained from a setback is confidence. I understand this might sound odd that losing might actually help you gain confidence, but if used properly, it can. For example, when I was starting out my career in sales, I bombed on my first few sales presentations . . . ok, I bombed on a lot of my initial sales presentations, but I was fresh into business, fresh into selling, and fresh into trying about almost everything in life. Even though I failed and lost those sales, I did something that was different than most. I analyzed the encounter and started to dissect what was working and what was not. Pretty soon, I started to realize what I was good at and where I was struggling. Once I realized that there were parts of the selling process that I did well, I felt confident in those areas. Once I improved on my weaker areas and saw progress, I gained even more confidence. Once I started selling well and then started earning sales awards, I became mega-confident. Losing or experiencing a setback is simply a way of life telling you that there is an element or component within the process that you're completing that needs to be modified and enhanced. You gain confidence by overcoming these areas of weakness and once you start to see progress and success in these areas, your confidence will explode and you will become unstoppable. UFC fighter Brock Lesnar once said, "Losing sucks. I hate to lose. You put in months of hard work training specifically to win a fight and then you fail. But everyone loses in this sport. It's how you pick yourself up after the loss that makes the difference."(45)

A weak person gets beat and decides to never pursue their dream again. A champion will take that which stopped them and learn to master it. They overcome the obstacle, master it, and make what was once a weakness, a proven talent or skill. Just like the old saying goes, that which does not kill you, will only make you stronger, and this statement resonates with truth.

RULES OF THE OCTAGON

Rule #7: Don't lose, but know how to manage and learn for a loss or setback if one occurs.

Remember, a loss can happen to even the best fighters, business professionals, leaders, and students. The loss does not matter as much as what the person does to manage and learn from the experience. But with that said, the best way to deal with a loss is to never have one or to greatly reduce your chances of experiencing the setback. We do that by focusing on the win and taking steps to increase our chances of earning the win. The following are some of the principles to use to create winning results.

- **Apply logic**: Using logic or thinking about the situation in detail is a great way to avoid simple mistakes and quick failures. Some people jump into a situation, fail miserably, and then afterwards say silly things such as, "In hindsight, I guess it wasn't a good idea," or "What was I thinking?" Let me give you an example of a situation that I saw happen, and use this scenario to determine if proper logic was applied when a decision was made. One of my best friends fought his first amateur mixed martial art fights last year in the 170 pounds weight class.

His average weight before taking the fight was above 190 pounds, so he was going to have to lose a lot of weight in order to fight, and lose weight is exactly what he did.

He dropped to 170 pounds with impressive fashion and was training hard for the bout. On the day that the weigh-ins occurred for his fight, his opponent showed up and weighed in at over 185 pounds. Now most fighters know that if you miss weight, it's probably by one pound or two pounds if your dieting had gone haywire, but to weigh in at over 15 pounds above the targeted weight class is just crazy.

My friend could have backed out of the fight and everyone would have understood and accepted his decision. Well, the thing about my friend is that he has the heart of a lion and balls of titanium, so he told his opponent to drop as much weight as he could in one day and weigh in one more time before the fight and he would make his final decision. Fight night came and his opponent still weighed around 181 pounds. My friend took the fight and it was an incredible bout. Round one had both fighters coming out and throwing some powerhouse punches that connected but neither fighter dropped. Later in the first round, both of the fighters started to tire, but made it to bell and were allowed to catch their breath and drink some water. Round two started and both of the fighters came out swinging. After a couple of minutes, both fighters became exhausted and finally the fight went to the ground. The guy fighting my friend was dead tired and he fell upon the cage, lying on his side trying to catch his breath. He then rolled over and lifted his right arm into the air for some reason. I was working in my friend's corner and I yelled, "Arm bar!"

An arm bar is a Brazilian Jiu Jitsu submission in which you lock your opponent's arm between your legs and you apply torque to the elbow as you lift your waist while locking down your opponent's arm. It's a very effective submission and if done right, you normally can get your opponent to tap out (quit) in seconds. My friend did not put his opponent in the arm bar, but he jumped on top of him and started to ground and pound (striking an opponent while you're on top of them) as best he could. He was seconds from winning the fight but then the bell rang. Round three started and both fighters were exhausted.

Punches were thrown but it was a total test of endurance. Finally the guy fighting my buddy hit him with a solid punch and the fight went back down to the ground. This time the opponent was able to do some ground and pound of his own and the fight was called due to referee stoppage.

Was it logical for my friend to fight a guy who outweighed him by close to fifteen pounds or should he have scrapped the fight because his opponent clearly was not disciplined to even make weight? Perhaps my friend looked at his opponent and calculated that if the guy was not disciplined enough to make weight, how good could his fighting style be? Also, if he beat this guy who outweighed him by so much, not only would he gain respect for the win, but also for the fact that he beat someone much bigger than he was during the fight. On the other hand, when you cut weight, it drains your strength and energy and thus you are prone to gas out or get tired faster. Perhaps another view from an analytical perspective would have said taking the fight with an opponent less likely to gas out because he did not cut weight may not have been the best idea?

In the case of my friend's fight, he did not get dominated and he earned mad respect from me and almost everyone in the crowd for putting on such a dynamic fight.

As you can tell from the scenario above, there are multiple points to consider regarding my friend's decision to take the fight. So how do you make a decision if there are multiple options, outputs, or factors to consider regarding the matter? One of the best techniques that I have used is an old process called the Ben Franklin Decision method or what some people call the Balance Sheet method.

The way the Ben Franklin Decision method works is you take a piece of paper and you draw an outline as such:

PROS	CONS

One the *pros* side of the grid, you list out the reasons why it's a good idea to do the thing you're thinking about. Really think about all of the positive options or positive data points that would make your decision or action a good one to make. Next, on the *cons* side of the grid, write down why it may not be a good idea to complete the action or decision you're considering. Again, really think about everything that might be a factor in making this decision a negative one.

Once completed, if you find that you have more pros than cons, the decision is sound and logical. If you find you have more cons than pros, then chances are that the choice or action is not one that will generate success for you. Whether it's with a simple solution such as the Ben Franklin Decision method or another way of logically analyzing you options, always look at the data that is available to ensure your decisions and actions are sound and will generate success for you.

- **Use the law of averages:** The law of averages is a theory that states after a given number of occurrences an average or pattern will emerge. In other words, if someone flips a coin ten times and it lands on heads four out of ten times, your law of average for the exercise is 40%. With that rule of thumb in mind, if you toss the coin ten more times, you should average at least 40% of the time on heads. Obviously, this is not an exact science, but if an activity that you're performing is cyclical in nature and you can count averages, then try to use the law of averages to see if you can generate some form of predictive data.

For example, if you're in sales and you close six out of ten presentations that you make, and you want to close at least twenty sales a week, the law of averages will tell you that you need to make forty presentations in a week and you should end up with approximately twenty-four sales. Forty presentations divided by five business days means you'll have to do on average eight presentations a day. The law of averages can be applied to almost any aspect of life, even dating.

If a guy gets one number for every five girls he talks to, he knows that he needs to talk to at least five girls when he goes out . . . and he needs to learn some new pick up lines. Use the law of averages to create predictions for your actions and use the averages to generate wins.

- **Train harder than the fight itself:** A proven way to increase your success in anything that you do is to train harder than what you'll have to perform during the actual task you're trying to accomplish. Many MMA fighters actually train to complete six rounds for three round fights, and some fighters like Dominick Cruz are known to train for ten rounds for their five round championship fights. There's an MMA training exercise called "shark tank" which pits a fighter against another fighter for one round, but at the start of the second round, a brand new opponent is brought in to fight. After the second round, a brand new opponent is also brought in to fight, and this continues for however many rounds the instructor is pushing the fighter to complete.

The fighter is tired after the first round, but is faced with an opponent who is fresh and ready to fight hard.

As you can imagine, this exercise is exhausting, and I've seen some fighters barely able to stand by the fourth round. When this fighter fights for real, he or she will have the cardio and energy required to complete the fight, and this time, will be fighting against someone who more than likely did not complete a "shark tank" exercise and this might result in a competitive advantage throughout the fight. If you train twice as hard as the event itself, your chances for success expand. If you only train for the exact or, worse, less than the exact amount of effort you'll need to exert, chances are that you're going to struggle.

If you're in business this means you practice your presentations repeatedly so you master your communication and presentation skills. If you're in sales, you practice your sales pitch repeatedly so you know exactly what you're going to say and how to address objectives if your clients have questions about your product or service. If you're a student, you study and drill for tests until you know the material like the back of your hand. Whatever it is that you do in life and/or in your profession, you master it and train twice as hard as the task itself. Another benefit of doing this is that pretty soon everything becomes easier and you find yourself able to go to the next level of success with greater ease. Also, be smart about your training. Hard work is not the key to success, hard and smart work is the key. Remember, hard training done right leads to greater development and accomplishments.

- **Remember your "why":** As discussed in chapter two, understanding and using the "why" principle, or the power that comes from harnessing the motivation to support the people and things you love, is a very powerful thing. Remember, what you do impacts those that you love and hold dearest to you. Your loss is their loss. That money you did not make when you did not close that sale, is money the people depending on you won't see. The bonus you missed by not making your company goals is going to be a bonus your family won't be able to use to vacation or pay for important things you're saving to purchase. Yeah, this fact sucks and it downright should piss you off, because you're working hard to take care of the things that are important to you, and they won't be taken care of if you don't win. But win you will, because you use the power of "why" and you use it in advance of completing the things you do. You use the power of knowing what's at stake when you train, when you perform, and when you need it the most. You never go into anything blind to what's at stake. You go into situations knowing that when you're done, the things you hold dearest to you will be that much better off. Remember to use the power of "why" during your planning and preparations. Know what's at stake and use what's at stake to quantify the impact. Knowing what's at stake will increase your chances of winning because you'll be fighting like hell to serve the things that mean the most to you.

- **Apply what you've learned (best practices):** An effective technique used in business is the process of identifying and utilizing best practices. Best practices are those actions or items that have been done that generate the greatest success. A delivery company may find best practices to be padding the inside of their delivery vehicles to reduce shipment damages by 40%. A restaurant may find a best practice is to use disposable and recyclable table cloths to reduce table clean up and furniture wear and tear by 27%. Each industry can have its own share of best practices and effective companies capture these because it allows them to be successful over and over again. If they had to design and develop solutions over and over again for things that they did in the past, chances are that they are going to deliver inconsistent results, as well as increase their costs of doing business.

Best practices aren't just for businesses though, and you can create your own set of best practices for success in anything that you do. The way you accomplish developing best practices is twofold. First, to capture your existing best practices, start to document the things that you do that are generating success. For example, if you found that you sold 20% more on the days when you cold called at least twenty businesses, and followed up with at least thirty emails, this is a best practice for you. If you're a fighter and find that you generate more success and win fights when you mix your training to include an intense cardio work out in the beginning, followed by thirty minutes of striking, thirty minutes of ground work, and thirty minutes of sparring, this is a best practice for you.

Your best practices can be as involved and as complex as detailing the exact diet, exercises, training, rest, and conditioning steps that you'll take before an upcoming fight, to something as simple as defining a best practice for paying bills.

The second way to develop and utilize best practices is to use what others have done to generate success. This can be other companies or other individuals, but simply do what they are doing to generate results and you'll share the same success. If you have a friend who makes the same amount of money that you do but she lives debt free, find out what her best practices are related to debt management and paying bills and you'll find yourself debt free in record time. If you're a student and there's someone you know who has a 4.0 grade point average, talk with this person and find out what best practices work for them and do what they're doing to generate the same results. Fighting is the same way. If there is someone at your MMA gym that is winning fights with dynamic results, find out what this person is doing as it relates to training, conditioning, and working out. Replicate this person's best practices and you'll start to see similar results. Remember, you don't have to invent or re-invent the wheel to generate successful results. Just capture what you're doing to generate success and keep doing it. If you're not generating positive results yourself, find someone who is and duplicate their best practices and start increasing your successes in record time.

- **Expect to win:** Expect to win sounds so simple and yet it's what many people fail to do. It drives me crazy when I hear things like "I hope I'll do well" or "I think I'll do ok." You have to KNOW that you're going to succeed. I tell my kids things like, "Of course you're going to do great, you're a Johnson!" and "You'll do well because it's part of your DNA!" I know they think I'm goofy, but if you say something enough, people start to believe it and then positive reinforcement of the idea starts to set in. You have to promote success in your mind and start expecting yourself to generate great results. Once you start to create some positive results with the things that you do, your mind will have all of the proof that it needs for validation and then your positive mental attitude will launch like a rocket. How many MMA fighters have you ever heard say things like, "Man, I'm more than likely going to get knocked out cold tonight" or "I'll give the guy less than a minute and I know he'll have me submitted?" Trust me, you'll never hear stuff like that, or at least not from someone who is a legitimate mixed martial artist. MMA fighters are confident in their skills and know they will win. They have to respect the power and skill of their opponent, but they know they have the ability to win the fight and they train and prepare for the fight with that confidence in mind. Regardless if you're in business or just entering high school, the more confident you are about generating and achieving success, the greater your chances will be of actually generating great results. Expect to win and soon enough you will win and win big.

THE SCORECARD

- *ALWAYS FIGHT TO WIN*
- *IF YOU DO EXPERIENCE A SETBACK, LEARN FROM IT*
- *USE LOSS AS A MOTIVATION TO WIN AND WIN BIG*
- *USE LOGIC TO INCREASE YOUR CHANCES OF WINNING*
- *TRAIN AND PREPARE HARDER THAN THE FIGHT ITSELF*
- *ALWAYS REMEMBER YOUR "WHY"*
- *USE THE PRACTICES THAT YOU OR OTHERS HAVE USED TO GENERATE SUCCESS*
- *EXPECT TO WIN!*

Harnessing the winning mind

"A champion is a champion because of what's inside of him. It's not because of anything else." Urijah Faber—*Fight* Magazine April 2010

THE WINNING MIND

The final and most critical stage of generating success in your life endeavors is to harness and maximize the use of a winner's mindset, or what some call the winning mind. The winning mind is the mental state that successful people develop in order to stay focused, positive, and clearly guided to generate extraordinary results. When an individual uses all of the techniques, solutions, and steps outlined in this book and they couple it with the power of training their mind to focus on success, they will be unstoppable. The reason why it is critical to possess a winning mind is because without strong focus on success and generating results, for some people, even if they know what to do to be successful, they either lack the discipline to complete the task or the tenacity to hang in there when work and hard effort is required. UFC President Dana White said it best when he said, "You have to be willing to do whatever it takes to win as long as it's fair and legal. I believe that some people are born with an insane will to win and some are not. Once someone has called me out or created a competition with me, then it becomes the only thing I think about.

I become 1,000 times more focused, and I literally don't stop until I win. I know I have to outwork, outmaneuver, outthink, and basically do everything better than them and make sure I beat them every day of the week until I win! I love being challenged. I believe it's what gets me out of bed every day. Life gets boring without it! I need it."(46)

For people who possess a winning mindset, not only do they have the mental faculties to achieve great results, their mind is also mentally programmed to get laser locked on achieving the objectives they are working to complete. Accomplishing results and achieving success is the dominant thought and driver that fuels the activities that they complete on a daily basis. Whether it's training, studying, or preparing for completing a task, the success-oriented individual uses the winning mind and the warrior's heart to bring their best to everything they do.

Some are born with the intestinal fortitude and cerebral firepower to automatically fuel and feed what was required in their life to achieve a winning mindset, and some of us have had to learn and grow along the way. The winning mind can be harnessed by anyone as long as they master a set of achievement principles and they follow the guidelines that have been covered in this book thus far. The achievement principles that I mentioned above are simple in their complexities, and yet powerful in their results. Anyone can achieve results by using them. Again, those who use them in conjunction with other foundations of success will achieve more, but even just using the achievement principles alone will set you apart from the norm and begin generating results for you once mastered.

THE S.U.C.C.E.S.S. SYSTEM

The achievement principles mentioned in this chapter are the components of a set of rules that I call the S.U.C.C.E.S.S. system. As much as I would like to think that it is, the S.U.C.C.E.S.S. system is not rocket science, and yet many people struggle on a daily basis because they fail to follow one or all of the elements of the S.U.C.C.E.S.S. system. If you follow these rules of success, I will guarantee you will see results in almost everything you do. If you couple the rules of the S.U.C.C.E.S.S. system with all of the lessons that I've covered in this book, you will be unstoppable. With that said, here are the individual rules of the S.U.C.C.E.S.S. system.

Success spawns success: You will notice that the more you focus on achieving results and generating success in your life, the more success and achievement will grow around you. Success is like a small snowball that you start rolling from the top of a very large hill. Once it starts, it begins to grow, and grow, until by the time it reaches the bottom of the hill, your snowball is huge. Once you start to build your success foundations, you'll start to notice how magazines you read help you grow. You'll notice that you start to learn from the people that you meet on a daily basis. You'll find that your desire for achievement will start to develop into other aspects of your life. Success spawns additional success.

One success will lead to another and then the next thing you'll know, what you thought was impossible or difficult to achieve will become common place. What you thought you could accomplish will be dwarfed by what you actually accomplish. At first you will start going to people for help and for guidance, and then they will start coming to you for help. When you help others, it actually helps you grow even more. What you give out comes back to you tenfold. Success manifests success in both yourself and in others. If you become the conduit for success and accomplishment, you will find that good things come to you and your achievements will be compounded. There is an old saying that states that "misery loves company," and while this is true, it is also true that success spawns success. Surround yourself with successful people. Do what successful people do and you will find success all around you. Once you achieve results, share your knowledge and skills to help others grow. Life is about reciprocity, so if you give, you will receive. Now this does not mean that once you've generated success you no longer have to work for additional success and that additional achievement is guaranteed, because nothing in life besides birth and death is guaranteed, but your momentum for generating success will have been activated, and what used to take you a lot of effort to generate results will now be easier to achieve and additional resources will be made available to you in the process. Always focus on success and allow the success and achievement that you generate to grow and spawn even greater results for yourself and the people around you.

Understand your strengths and weakness: A powerful person is one that realizes there are things that you do in your life that are clearly a core competency for you, and there are things that you need to improve upon, or are current challenges for you. Having a weakness or a challenge is not a problem, but not identifying, not understanding, and not working to improve your areas of weakness are the mistakes to avoid. An effective MMA fighter will analyze his or her areas of fighting skills and will look for the areas that need improvement. For example, a fighter might be a division 1 wrestler but have limited boxing, Jiu Jitsu, or Muay Thai skills and will identify these as areas of weakness or improvement, and thus they focus on getting better in those areas. The fighter will continue to work on the areas that are their strengths, but focus will be applied to the areas where they need to improve in order to become a more effective individual.

. This same principle applies in all aspects of life. If you're starting a new business and you don't take inventory of your strengths and weaknesses, you're probably in for a huge eye-opening experience, or worse, potential failure to successfully run your business. If your past business experience was in sales, you probably have the required skills to market the product or service you're offering in your new business, but what about accounting and bookkeeping? What about managing people? What about handling customer satisfaction issues?

An effective person will review their skills and identify that they need help in certain areas and they will either start to gain the required experience and education in this area, or they will find people to work with who have strengths in that particular area. You might not have any desire to understand bookkeeping in your new business, but you at least want to understand the basics and then hire a professional to handle the actual task so the function is successfully completed. A best practice performed by many of today's successful corporations is the completion of formal training to properly assess employee strengths and weakness, as well as implement advanced training to groom these individuals for future company success. An example of this is, before a person can be considered for a Vice Presidency position within a firm, they must first work in all divisions of the company, and they must complete advanced negotiation, accounting, management, customer satisfaction, and leadership training. The training and time-in-rank for the job experience is tracked and becomes part of the consideration for candidates filling future executive positions. This allows the employee to grow and expand their strengths in the areas where they might be lacking training and experience.

Early in my career, most of my experience was in sales. I wanted to grow within my company but then I started to hear things such as, "You're just a sales guy" which basically meant that people did not think I had enough operational experience to move up within the company.

To address this situation, I started to shift my career focus to begin working in operations and project management. There is a world of difference between sales and operations, but they both need each other and when you have skills in both areas, you become even more effective. At the end of the day, I'm a sales guy but I can also say that I have operational experience, I've managed people, know how to read a profit and loss statement, create, follow, and cut a budget to meet company goals, and I know how to address customer satisfaction situations. Am I perfect in business? Hell no, and even today I analyze my areas of strength and areas of weakness that need improvement. The day you stop growing or trying to grow is the day you start being stale and obsolete. The best way to understand your strengths and weaknesses is to create what is known as a S.W.O.T. analysis. S.W.O.T. stands for strengths, weaknesses, opportunities, and threats. Using the new business owner example mentioned above, this individual's S.W.O.T. analysis might look something like this.

Strengths	Opportunities
Sales, Marketing, Advertising	Hire accountant and part-time bookkeeper. Take a class at local university to understand business finance, management, and operations.

Weaknesses	Threats
Accounting, Operations, Scheduling, Managing People.	Mismanage money and not be able to pay bills. Lose business or fail to gain new clients because of operational issues.

S.W.O.T. allows you to identify the areas where you should be covered, as well as your areas of weakness and the potential impact of the weaknesses or challenges if not addressed. Creating a S.W.O.T. is a simple task to complete and it allows you to see the things you need to work on to increase your chances of generating successful results.

Remember, acknowledging that there are areas that you need to improve upon is not a sign of weakness, but rather a sign of strength and maturity. Understanding that you can make these areas of weakness a future strength, as well as remind yourself that you are already strong in other areas, is the way you develop and grow as an individual in a positive and powerful way.

Change past conditions causing failure: Success is generated when a defined and proven set of actions are presented to an individual with the passion and motivation to succeed. Likewise, failure and challenges are presented to those that continue to follow a path or actions that have caused them past failures. Have you ever known anyone who said things such as, "When I get drunk, I always get in trouble," or "I keep getting fired for not showing up to work?" There are people who continue to repeat the same errors in life and can't seem to figure out why they continue to face challenges and failures. Even more concerning is many of these people actually know that what they're doing is going to cause them issues and yet they follow the same path to failure.

Some conditions are serious and are part of severe situations such as addiction and mental disorders, but other conditions can be avoided by simply taking action to understand the impact of the action and why you should be avoiding it. Addictions and disorders should be treated by a doctor or a trained professional in that field, but if you find yourself experiencing challenges in certain areas of your life, examine the actions that you are taking and determine if you are repeating past conditions and actions that have been causing you issues for some time. If you find yourself repeatedly getting fired from jobs, honestly look at what you are doing that might be causing the situations. Make a list of what you feel might be root cause issues and specify what you're going to do to now take action to rectify them and not repeat them. In the case of the person who continuously loses his job, he might find his list looking something like this:

1.) Stay up late at night and then I sleep in past my alarm clock.
2.) Arrive late to work and leave as soon as I can.
3.) Give the boss attitude when they talk about my work ethics.
4.) Spend my paycheck as soon as I get it and then have to borrow money until the next pay check.

Obviously, this person has a lot to work on, but at least he went through the efforts of making the list of items that he feels are past and continuous issues causing him failure.

Once the list of items has been completed, he would then take the list and apply a positive go-forward plan on how he would rectify the situations and discontinue performing the actions. His list might now look like this:

1.) Every night I go to bed at 10:00 p.m. and set two alarms for the morning.

2.) I will arrive 30 minutes early to work each day and I will leave 30 minutes after my shift. I will be the first to arrive and the last to leave.

3.) I will complete high caliber work, but if my performance is measured in a manner where I'm given advice on areas of improvement, I will listen, show appreciation for the feedback, and take actions to exceed expectations.

4.) I will create a budget and my extra income will be deposited into a savings account.

After this new set of actions has been defined and implemented, the individual in our example would need to monitor the results that he generates after completing the steps. Perhaps he might have to tweak a step or two, but chances are that he will generate results that are far more productive than his past situations, and after a period of time, these new actions become habit. The period of time that it takes for a new action to become a habit is different for each person, but it is said that on average, a new habit is formed after twenty-one days of performing a new process.

The new steps might be difficult or cumbersome at first, but once success has been generated, positive motivation will be tied to the steps and a new positive habit is formed. Always monitor your actions when challenges arise and determine if you are repeating steps that are causing you issues. Once you identify the actions, discontinue them, create positive counter-actions, and watch your results change for the better.

Change your associations with pleasure: Imagine this situation. A man and a woman are arguing because the man saw the woman talking to another man. After the man gets angry, he puts his fist through the window in his apartment. The woman sees that the man's hand is now cut from the window and she wraps up his wound. Afterwards, she holds him and tells him he shouldn't be so angry and then they make passionate love. Subconsciously, what mental associations do you think this man's mind is making from this experience? How about things such as anger equals sex, or smashing things equals eventual love? So the next time this couple argues, what do you think the chances are that this guy will try to smash something again? Your brain is attracted to the things that it associates with pleasure, and regardless of how absurd the action is, if you generate pleasure from it, you will do it. A prime example of this happened to me in high school when I hung around a bunch of kids who liked to smoke. Every morning a group of us would get together before school and the "cool" kids of the group would be smoking.

I wanted to fit in, so I decided to try smoking myself. I thought that surely the cigarettes would taste good because everyone was smoking them and they seemed to really enjoy the experience. I lit up my first cigarette and put it to my mouth, ready to enjoy the new experience of smoking. Then something unexpected happened. I inhaled the smoke and started to cough. The smoke itself tasted like a turd-sandwich, and I could not stop coughing. Then I got real light headed and felt dizzy for several minutes. So obviously, that was the last time I ever smoked right? Wrong. I continued to smoke because smoking meant that I was part of the group and I associated pleasure with this experience. Then I got hooked on cigarettes and that was a whole other topic of odd pleasure association. Finally, after I joined the Navy, I quit smoking but then I met a girl who smoked and she let me try one of her cigarettes. When I smoked the cigarette she commented that I looked cool, and with that, my second round of cigarette addiction started. Eventually, I stopped smoking (permanently!) but that experience taught me that people will do some crazy things when they associate something positive or pleasurable with an action.

Successful people look to associate pleasure with positive and powerful things that serve them, as well as others. A successful person will feel pleasure when she donates a percentage of her company profits to help out underprivileged children. A successful person will feel pleasure when he associates working out at the gym with maximizing his health. A successful person will feel pleasure when he spends time with his wife and children and works to ensure they understand that they are important to him.

When you evaluate the progress that you've made, always review how and with what you are associating pleasure in life. If some things are not serving you or others, make changes. Life is about constant adjustment and evaluating your status and progress. If what you're doing will cause more harm than good, make adjustments. No one is perfect and yet you'll be as perfect as you can be if you identify and understand what motivates and drives you. Some things you do might be completely useless, and yet make logical sense. For example, I love to play video games. I'll spend hours playing games that don't really serve me in any particular way other than allowing me to take a break and have some fun. We all need our diversions and for me, a good video game or playing my drums does that. I look at those things as exercises in mental health. If you review your actions, you might find situations like this as well, but as long as you can see the positive aspects of them and they are not harming you or others, continue what brings you pleasure. Again, if the action is negative and harms yourself or others, this is what you must discontinue. Associating pleasure with the positive things that serve you and bring you the most success is a major key to achieving results and living your life with purpose.

Expect to achieve results and a high level of output from yourself: "I get my tireless work effort from my Mom and Dad. They have always instilled in me that hard work will pay off in the long run. I truly believe this, as I have seen the fruits of my labor when my hand is raised after a hard fought battle. I also try to instill this in my teammates, fans, and future MMA fighters when they ask me where I get my cardio, or how do I fight so hard, for so long. I tell them hard work will take you very far in your everyday life, not just sports."(47) is a quote from UFC fighter Clay Guida, and one that best exemplifies the intensity and passion by which one who is looking to achieve results in life must live. Successful people don't hope or wish for the achievement of high caliber performance and results, they expect it from themselves. It's a given that great things will happen when planning, hard work, and passion meet up. Successful people know that everyone has "off" days, and everyone will experience setbacks from time to time, but they use these experiences to learn and to go back to battle with even more intensity and focus than before.

Your brain is like an advanced computer that runs on a set of programs that you feed it on a daily basis. In the world of software programming, there is an understanding that "garbage in, equals garbage out," which basically states that if you add junk code into a program, you get junk results. The same is applicable with mental programming. Your mind will achieve what you tell it to achieve. If you limit yourself by programming your mind with limited or negative thoughts, limited or negative results are what you will achieve. Garbage in equals garbage out.

It takes some time and focus, but you can condition yourself to become cognizant of your internal programming and you can work to remove and replace negative thoughts with positive thoughts that generate success.

Less effective people only think about negative things and how life is working against them. Effective people re-program their minds to expect high impact results and if something negative does happen, they relate this event to a life lesson or opportunity to gain experience. It all starts in the mind and with the programming that we feed it on a daily basis. Here are some examples of common negative thoughts and how effective people re-program the thoughts to generate positive results.

Negative Programming Examples:

1. "Another Monday, and another day of having to deal with this stupid job."
2. "This test is going to be hard. I know I'm going to flunk it."
3. "I'm so weak. There's no way I'll ever be able to run on the treadmill for more than ten minutes."
4. "I'll never be able to make any money."
5. "There's no way I'm making this sale today."
6. "Life sucks. Everyone's doing well except for me. I'm such a loser."

Positive Programming Replacements:

1. "Yes! I have a job when many don't and I'm going to work hard today and achieve great things."
2. "This test is advanced and a sign that I'm learning more. I've studied hard for it and will pass with flying colors."
3. "I know that working out takes time and I'm committed to building my body into its optimum shape. Health is important to me and I will do what is required to achieve my fitness goals. Pain is simply weakness leaving the body."

4. "Wealth is in my future. I know the harder and smarter that I work, the more money will flow to me. As I make money, I save it and invest it into things that will make me even more money in the future."

5. "I deliver the best customer satisfaction and my product/ service is the best in the industry. I will make this sale and I will generate additional referrals from the client in the process."

6. "Life is an incredible gift. Every day, I have the opportunity to live, love, and prosper. I will take advantage of what today offers and I will commit to giving it my all."

Successful Programming When a Setback Occurs:

1. **Lost sale:** "Sales is a numbers game. I will take this situation and review what I could have done better, and I'll move on to next client. The more clients I talk to today, the more sales I will make."

2. **Missed Fitness Goal:** "I'm doing great by going to the gym and eating right, and I will take my intensity to the next level. I will conquer my fitness goals and I welcome the intensity of the work out. Pain is just a sign that my body is developing."

3. **Lost competition:** "I competed to the best of my abilities today. I learned from this experience and I will use this lesson to train harder and achieve success in the future."

4. **Missed Financial Goal:** "I will achieve my financial goals. This setback is just a lesson for me to learn and something to avoid in the future. I am a rich person mentally and I know my efforts will generate financial benefits in the very near future."

Several years ago when I first started to consciously listen to the thoughts that were going through my mind, I was floored at how much negative programming was going on. I was subconsciously creating barriers for myself and limiting my true capabilities. It took some effort but I worked to stop the negative thought mid-stream and immediately replace it with a positive command. For me, this was an exercise that I had to do for several months and to this day, I have to watch what I'm thinking at times. I think it's human nature to think negative by default, and perhaps this is a primal condition that kept our Cro-Magnon ancestors from getting eaten by Saber-toothed tigers ("Hey, I bet there's a mammoth in that cave! Maybe I shouldn't go in there?"), but today it limits the capabilities and potential for a very large percentage of our population. When you program your mind for success, you generate success. When your mind is expecting to generate high impact results, your body will follow. Allow your brain to remove its negative barriers and open yourself to generating positive results that you are capable of producing in your life.

Always push yourself physically and mentally and expect great things from yourself. You'll be shocked to see what you're capable of doing when it comes to achieving greatness.

T.K.O. (Tips, Knowledge, and Objectives)

If you're interested in learning more about subconscious reprogramming and creating positive conscious thoughts for greater success, I would recommend picking up the book "Passion, Profit, and Power" by Marshall Sylver. This book had a tremendous impact on my early professional career and Marshall is now offering additional material on topics ranging from persuasion training to using hypnosis to lose weight and quit smoking. You can order the book and learn more about Marshall at www.sylver.com.

Stay away from negative influences: As mentioned above, negative thinking and programming can wreak havoc on people's lives and truly limit them to subpar performance in life, but negative influences can expand well beyond just mental conditions. Negative influences have the capability of infiltrating all aspects of our lives. Some of the more common negative influences to avoid include:

1. **Limited-minded people with negative outlooks on life:** There are people who put more effort in trying to limit other people's lives than they do trying to improve their lives. These people are dream-killers and throw water on the flames of people who are trying to generate success in life.

   These are the people who tell you negative things and try to bring you down to their levels in an effort to prevent you from generating success and taking it away from them.

   Remember, there is a huge difference between someone with experience giving you advice (which might seem like negative feedback) compared to the person who is simply trying to kill your dream ("You'll never be anything in life!") so remove yourself from these influences and surround yourself with people who build your dream and provide you with support.

In the World of MMA, there are several teams that are formed that serve the purpose of training elite fighters, as well as provide a support mechanism for these fighters to grow physically and mentally. Urijah Faber's "Team Alpha Male" is a prime example of this type of support mechanism. Team Alpha Male showcases some of the best current and up and coming MMA fighters in Sacramento, California, and provides members with access to advanced training and guidance from fighters who are currently generating solid results in mixed martial arts. The type of people with whom you surround yourself become the type of person you'll likely develop into. Be sure to surround yourself with positive and powerful people working to achieve results and help you grow as a person.

2. **Drugs and Alcohol Abuse:** As someone who enjoys the occasional glass of wine or beer, I'm not against alcohol or anything like that, but I also realize that any intake of alcohol or any drug for that matter, can negatively impact my performance.

I've had less than optimal workouts because I decided to get "loose" the night before and drink a beer or four with my buddies. So if you decide to drink, you should expect your performance to be impacted. If you're cool with that, then the decision is yours, but realize the less you subject yourself to drinking and smoking situations, they better your output will be in general. Drug and alcohol abuse is a serious situation and is not something to be taken lightly. As a person that comes from a family with a history of challenges with drugs and alcohol, I've personally seen the negative things that can come from substance abuse. If you suffer from substance abuse now, I would highly encourage you to seek professional help and remove this negative element from your life. You don't have to abuse substances because people in your family did. You can gain control over the situation and run your life on your terms. Just realize that there is a substantial difference between the occasional drinker and someone who blacks out during drunken episodes multiple times a week. If your drinking or smoking is out of control, seek help and grow beyond this negative inhibitor.

3. **The News and Media**: If you ever want to get depressed, angry, and down on life in general, just pick up a newspaper, news magazine, watch the news, or visit a news website. It's good to stay informed on things going on in our world, but for some reason the media wants to educate us by fear and anger. They say that sex sells, but I think fear and anger is an equally matched selling mechanism.

Limit what you expose yourself to on a daily basis, as well as how long you expose yourself to it. Personally, I'll check a couple of news websites in the morning and that's about it. I no longer subscribe to the newspaper and I don't watch the nightly news on TV. I try to limit my exposure to the media and to things that I don't control (but that want to control me). If you make this one simple change in your life, you'll quickly start to see an adjustment in your outlook and overall perception.

We can't control all things in life, but we can reduce or eliminate the things that expose us to negative influences and negative situations. Make the commitment and the changes today to focus on the positive aspects of life and remove the things in your life that cause negativity. Your output and results are a direct reflection of the things with which you surround yourself. Make sure you surround yourself with success and people/things there to serve you and help you to achieve results.

Study under those who have generated success: Having the influence of a coach, a trainer, a mentor, or even another individual who has achieved success can be the fuel that powers your success to the next level. NFL coach Tom Landry once said, "A coach is someone who tells you what you don't want to hear, who has you see what you don't want to see, so you can be who you have always known you could be."(48)

A good coach can make or break you. Note that I said a good coach can make or break you. Having a bad coach or trainer can be just as bad as not seeking any guidance at all. I once knew a fitness trainer who didn't push his clients at all during their workouts. He spent time talking about their weekends, their families, what was going on at work, etc. When they complained that the weight was getting a little heavy, he reduced it to an easier level. He probably kept a few clients that way because they could say they were using a personal trainer, but they really were not getting pushed or coached to the next level of success. The fitness trainers that I work with now beat the living tar out of me during workouts, and I actually enjoy the experience (crazy, I know!). In addition to my weekly fitness boot camp and strength training, my MMA classes all start with a thirty to forty minute intense cardio workout. By the end of the week, my body is ready to collapse on the coach and not move all weekend, but at the end of week I feel really good about my efforts and I look forward to the coming week to do it all over again. My trainers and Sensei are good at what they do and they make a big difference in my life.

Good coaching in the world of mixed martial arts is critically important. A good MMA coach can literally mean the difference between an ok fighter compared to a world class fighter. MMA coaches such as Trevor Wittman and Greg Jackson are two examples of individuals who know how to push fighters to their next level of success, and they do so using positive motivation driven by intense focus.

You can get a man or a woman to do incredible things if you know how to activate their motivations and passion. When you know how to motivate people and you do it in a positive and powerful way, you get even better results. You don't just build fighters, you build champions. The world of business and academics is the exact same way. A good professor can make the difference between a decent student compared to someone who earns Summa Cum Laude status. A good business coach can make the difference between making Vice President compared to making CEO. If you study under "F" students, you'll probably only get "F" grades. If you study under a business coach that has bankrupted multiple companies, you'll probably go bankrupt. It's a simple concept to comprehend and yet many people choose to follow negative role models or don't seek out any guidance at all. Keep powerful and positive people around you and seek the guidance of people who have generated past success. Train and learn from the best and when you have the opportunity to learn from greatness, always be respectful and show appreciation for the experience. People don't have to share their experience and knowledge with you, but sharing experience and knowledge is a sign of strength and maturity, as well as appreciation for others.

Give back to those who give to you and once you yourself have earned a degree of success, commit to sharing with others who are asking for assistance from you. As I mentioned before, life is reciprocal. What you give you get back, so give a lot and show appreciation for those who help you. Always remember, if you learn from the best, you achieve the best, so seek out good coaches, trainers, and people with knowledge to help you succeed.

RULES OF THE OCTAGON

Rule #8: Develop and Master the Winning Mind

Harnessing the winning mind is the ultimate tool in your arsenal of solutions and methods that will help you generate success and achievement in your life. Without the winning mind there is only luck and randomness. A mind focused on achieving excellence backed by hardcore work ethics are the ingredients for phenomenal results and unparalleled success. Some of the most successful people that I have known were individuals who were laser-locked on achieving goals and generating success.

I believe that the world of MMA offers so many examples of individuals who possess the winning mind, and the results of their hard work, dedication, and focus can be seen in the belt rankings that they have achieved, the bouts that they have won, how they conducted themselves after a loss, and ultimately, the championships that they have won along the way. I also believe that the world of MMA offers two additional elements of success that highly compliment the winning mind, and these two components of success are missing in many aspects, industries, and facets of life these days.

RESPECT AND HONOR

The first element of success that compliments the winning mind is a focus on nobility, respect, and honor. A true martial artist is not a street thug looking to jump into a cage in hopes of beating someone senseless. A true martial artist respects his or her opponent and they understand the nobility and honor that fighting represents. MMA represents a tangible and quantitative way for an individual to truly measure his or her progress in their chosen area of discipline. MMA is not a team sport; it's man against man, or woman against woman. After a fight or even a sparring session, an individual clearly knows their level of achievement and how well they are progressing within their discipline. Respect and nobility is woven within the fabric of MMA because martial arts has always been about respect and nobility. A student at a dojo bows before entering the training area and before class starts.

The individual who is success focused and conducts themselves in a noble and respectful way is a true warrior of success. This is a key differentiator between successful people and high impact successful people. Successful people who respect and honor those around them and the fruits of their labor will enjoy life to a degree that an average person will never see. The power of nobility and honor is immense and yet dormant in so many areas of everyday life. In recent years we've seen example after example of companies and individuals who have conducted themselves in ways that are not noble and honorable.

Be it examples such as Enron or Ponzi scheme artists like Bernie Madoff, both are illustrations of entities that have negatively impacted thousands of lives because of their greed and arrogance. A noble and honorable company will not take advantage of their customers and employees. A noble and honorable person will not take advantage or disrespect others. Noble and honorable people will conduct themselves in ways that bring positive light on them, their families, and the organizations that they represent.

Every one of us has the traits of nobility and honor, but not all of us will choose to exhibit these traits on a daily basis. The enlightened individual who possesses the winning mind and who is respectful, honorable, and noble with actions and intentions, is a powerful individual. They are the kind of person that has gained success and the people around them celebrate in their success. These are the people who have other people say things such as, "They deserve all the great things they get in life," and "That couldn't have happened to a better person." You see, anyone can become successful and achieve results in life, but a noble and honorable person who achieves success does so in a manner where others want to see them grow and are happy that they are prospering. Also, these people define and establish a future path of success for their families and associates. In many cultures, the children of nobility and honor are automatically accepted as honorable and noble citizens simply because of their lineage and ancestry. Remember, what you do and how you conduct yourself counts not only for generating your success, but how people support you once you're successful. Always be honorable and noble in your actions and intentions.

DEVELOPMENT OF A STRONG WORK ETHIC

If you ever think training in mixed martial arts is easy, I implore you to take an MMA class at a gym close to your home. I think you'll quickly find that MMA is the hardest, sweatiest, most painful fun that you'll ever have. Even those like myself, who only train in MMA for the fitness and knowledge of the sport, understand that you have to have a strong work ethic to achieve results in MMA. Professional mixed martial artists take the concept of a strong work ethic to a whole new level of ridiculousness. Many fighters work out two, if not three times a day. They watch their diets down to the calorie focus, and many work this crazy regimen while also working at other jobs and/or taking care of families. If you don't have a super strong work ethic in MMA, chances are that you're not going to succeed.

This same concept is true in almost every aspect of life. A strong work ethic will carry you to distances far greater than almost anything else in life. If you're not willing to work for what you want, I can almost guarantee you'll never achieve the level of success you were meant to achieve. You might get lucky here and there and you might achieve something if it's handed to you, but you'll only achieve a fragment of the true degree of success you would have achieved if you truly put forth effort. There's a quote by an unknown author that states, "All the so-called 'secrets of success' will not work unless you do."(49) I agree with this saying and the only thing I would add to the end of that sentence is the word "intelligently."

217

Whatever you do, do it intelligently. You see, it's not hard work that generates results; it's intelligent work that creates results. If two guys decide to build a wall and one guy carries his fifty pound bricks uphill by hand, while the other guy rents a bulldozer that does the work in a fraction of the time, which example is better? Both individuals worked, but one man worked substantially harder to generate results that took way longer than the other guy. Also, the man who carried the bricks by hand was probably left with a severe backache afterwards. You have to do the work, but you always need to work smart. Work your ass off . . . intelligently. Also, there is a hidden benefit or reward in the work. Football legend Vince Lombardi once said, "I firmly believe that any man's finest hour, the greatest fulfillment of all that he holds dear, is that moment when he has worked his heart out in a good cause and lies exhausted on the field of battle, victorious."(50) There is a feeling of pride and accomplishment that people feel when they take a step back and look at the achievements and progress of their efforts. Large or small, the effort can make us feel good about what we're doing and what we've achieved.

Hard and intelligent work is a key differentiator between those who just generate sub-par results and those who create dynamic accomplishments. I've personally seen people with only a high school education work circles around college graduates with MBA degrees. The difference was the high school graduate knew that they had to work their ass off to prove themselves but the MBA felt they deserved the success because they sat in a class room and read books.

I'm a big fan of academics, but I'm a bigger fan of someone who will bust their butt to generate results versus those who think they are better simply because of classroom time. Now, an MBA graduate who also rolls up his or her sleeves and gets down to work while using their brains, that's an incredible combination of success there. When I was studying to complete my MBA, there was a student in one of my classes who told me that she was quitting her job once she earned her MBA because while her company would pay for her classes, she would not be getting an immediate raise once she graduated. She told me, "I'll be an MBA soon and I expect MBA pay." Personally, I think she missed the whole point. Yes, she worked hard to earn her MBA, but her company invested in her and they obviously saw a benefit to increasing her education. I'm sure that if she earned her degree and applied that knowledge and her work ethic towards achieving a promotion at work, she would have earned the pay increase she felt she deserved. Unfortunately, she felt she deserved the reward without the effort and thus her company was now investing in an individual they would soon be losing, and more than likely, if she did go to a new company she would be unhappy for some reason or another.

Great things come to those who are willing to do the work. MMA is a sport that demands incredible work ethics and a commitment to working at a pace that would break lesser dedicated individuals. If you work at an output that is unmatched by anyone else, and you do so with intelligence and focus, your efforts will carry you far beyond what you see others generating in life. When someone goes an inch, you go a mile.

When they sell two cars, you sell twenty. When they turn in a ten page report, you turn in a fifteen page report with graphics. No one outworks you or outsmarts you.

Your work ethic is unmatched and is a primary reason for your success, and you find that the more you work, the easier the work becomes and the more you generate. Work is just like working out. If you've never curled a weight before, twenty-five pounds might feel heavy at first, but the more you work out, the stronger you get. Eventually, twenty-five pounds becomes easy, then forty-five pounds becomes easy, then sixty-five pounds becomes easy. The more you work, the better you get and the more you achieve. Always commit to putting in the effort it takes to succeed in life and do so in a way that achieves results for you and the goals you're looking to achieve.

THE SCORECARD

- *DEVELOP AND UTILIZE THE WINNING MIND*
- *UNDERSTAND THAT SUCCESS SPAWNS SUCCESS*
- *KNOW YOUR STRENGTHS AND WEAKNESSES*
- *CHANGE PAST CONDITIONS CAUSING FAILURE*
- *EXPECT TO ACHIEVE INCREDIBLE RESULTS*
- *STAY AWAY FROM NEGATIVE INFLUENCES*
- *STUDY UNDER THOSE WHO HAVE GENERATED SUCCESS*
- *ALWAYS SHOW HONOR, RESPECT, AND NOBILITY*
- *WORK HARD . . . INTELLIGENTLY*

Conclusion

When the gates are opened, the Octagon has a start and a finish, an entrance and an exit. When the gates are closed the shape is consistent, continuous, and constant. Life, and generating success in life, is very much the same way. When working to achieve results, you have to remain consistent, continuous, and constant, or you generate inconsistent and unpredictable results. The sides of the Octagon are defined steps to follow and elements of success to complete that will generate results.

Create Your Vision

Harness the
Winning Mind

Know Your "Why"

Learn From Failure

Eliminate Your Fear

Become a Leader

Be Persistent
and Never Quit

Dedicate Yourself
to Excellence

As you enter the Octagon, you come prepared with knowing why you're there and what you wish to accomplish. For some it's to win a battle with a fellow warrior. For others it's to generate business or academic success. For others, it's just a way of life. The path they choose while living a life of "carpe diem" or seizing the day. Every day is a day focused on achieving incredible results and accomplishments.

You now are aware of the sides of the Octagon and the steps within each side that you must complete in order to generate the success that you're looking to achieve in life. You now hold the power of understanding what's at stake for not working to achieve all of the things that you were meant to accomplish during your time on Earth.

I personally believe that we're all gifted with individual skills, talents, and a purpose to fulfill during our life. The road has been paved for us, but we're responsible for starting and finishing the journey. Some of us know exactly what has to be done in order to achieve our life's journey and we have the skills to complete the tasks. Others need a little boost and some guidance along the way. I hope that this book was the boost that you needed and now you're skyrocketing towards your dreams. I hope this book was the guidance that you needed to put you on a path that will find you creating remarkable things in your life. I know that when you enter your own Octagon and you begin your journey, the things you will accomplish will be of benefit and a gift to all of us, so start succeeding and start sharing today.

I want to hear about your success and what you've been able to accomplish by using the material in this book. Please visit my site at www.mmafighterconnect.com and send me your story at tony. johnson@mmafighterconnect.com.

In closing, the sport of MMA is growing by leaps and bounds, but is still nowhere close to the size that it will be in the next ten years. The sport needs the fans to help it grow to the next level. As the fans of MMA, we are the ones who will help it become the #1 sport on a local and international level. If you're an MMA fan now, you need to grab your friends and turn them into MMA fans as well. I owe my love for MMA to my friend, Hobert Blackburn, who told me I should start watching cage fights. At first I thought the idea was goofy and I wasn't even convinced I liked MMA when I finally did watch a fight. My friend then told me to give it another try and watch one more fight. All it took was that one extra MMA event to light the spark for me, and now I can't get enough of MMA. Do your friends this same favor and get them addicted to MMA. They'll thank you later.

Success to you,

Reference

1. "Tristin Carter," "Fighter Motivated by Award Winners," My Town Crier, June 28, 2011, accessed November 6, 2011, http://www.mytowncrier.ca/fighter-motivated-by-award-winners.html

2. "10 things to know about the UFC," accessed November 5, 2011, http://www.ufc.com/discover/fan

3. "Napoleon Hill Quotes," Think Exist, accessed November 5, 2011, http://thinkexist.com/quotation/cherish_your_visions_and_your_dreams_as_they_are/14325.html

4. Brian J. D'Souza, "The Quest For Perfection," Fight! Magazine, April, 2010

5. "Gian Carlo Menotti Quotes," Think Exist, accessed November 5, 2011, http://thinkexist.com/quotation/hell_begins_on_the_day_when_god_grants_us_a_clear/198861.html

6. "Where there is no vision, there is no hope," Quotations Book, accessed November 5, 2011, http://quotationsbook.com/quote/19421/

7. "The Way of Lao-Tzu" The Quotations Page, accessed November 5, 2011, http://www.quotationspage.com/quote/24004.html

8. Brian Knapp, "Golden Boy," Ultimate MMA Magazine, December, 2010, accessed July 5, 2011, http://www.ultimatemmamag.com/news/cover-story/2651-golden-boy

9. Joshua Carey, "Exclusive Interview with Greg Jackson: Mixed Martial Arts Premier Coach," Bleacher Report, April 30, 2010, accessed July 10, 2011, http://bleacherreport.com/articles/386264-exclusive-interview-with-greg-jackson-mixed-martial-arts-premier-coach

10. Zig Zigler, "Secrets of Closing the Sale" The Quotations Page, accessed November 5, 2011, http://www.quotationspage.com/quote/25955.html

11. "Maslow's Hierarchy of Needs" Dina Mehta, accessed January 10, 2011, http://dinamehta.com/blog/wp-content/uploads/2007/10/800px-maslows_hierarchy_of_needssvg.png

12. "Ultimate Fighting Quotes and Quotations" accessed November 5, 2011, http://www.mmawild.com/ufc/quotes/

13. Dale Carnegie, Quotations Book, accessed November 6, 2011, http://quotationsbook.com/quote/14724/

14. Franklin D. Roosevelt, "Only Thing We Have to Fear is Fear Itself—FDR's First Inaugural Address," History Matters, accessed November 5, 2011, http://historymatters.gmu.edu/d/5057/

15. Walter Cronkote, "Increase Your Confidence" Student Learning Commons, accessed November 5, 2011, http://learningcommons.sfu.ca/sites/default/files/218/presentations-increase.pdf

16. "Ultimate Fighting Quotes and Quotations" accessed November 5, 2011, http://www.mmawild.com/ufc/quotes/

17. Thomas Gerbasi, "Chasing Destiny," April 25, 2006, accessed December 10, 2010, www.diegonightmare.com/articles.html

18. "The Invisible Gorilla," Christopher Chabris and Daniel Simons, accessed December 1, 2010, www.theinvisiblegorilla.com

19. Napoleon Hill, "Think and Grow Rich," Combined Registry Company. P. 14

20. Norman Vincent Peale, "Laura Moncur's Motivational Quotations" The Quotations Page, accessed November 5, 2011, http://www.quotationspage.com/quote/2798.html

21. Eleanor Roosevelt, "Laura Moncur's Motivational Quotations" The Quotations Page, accessed November 5, 2011, http://www.quotationspage.com/quote/2558.html

22. Miguel Torres, "Modern-Day Superman" Fight! Magazine, August 2010, accessed on January 9, 2011, http://www.fightmagazine.com/mma-magazine/mma-article.asp?aid=572&issid=39

23. Doug Jeffrey, "Jorge Gurgel's Fight Camp," Ultimate MMA, March 2010

24. "Lance Armstrong Quotes" Think Exist, accessed November 5, 2011, http://thinkexist.com/quotation/pain_is_temporary-it_may_last_a_minute-or_an_hour/346310.html

25. Mark Gilbert, "Dana White has confirmed Chuck Liddell will never fight in the UFC again," May 1, 2009, accessed February 11, 2010, http://www.thesun.co.uk/sol/homepage/sport/ufc/article2407447.ece

26. Robert Burns, "No Takedown," Success Magazine, February 2011, P. 36

27. Dana White, "Inspirational Business Quotes" Evan Carmichael, accessed November 5, 2011, http://www.evancarmichael.com/blog/famous-quotes/inspirational-business-quotes/

28. Charles F. Horne, ed., The Sacred Books and Early Literature of the East, (New York: Parke, Austin, & Lipscomb, 1917), Vol. VI: Medieval Arabia, pp. 241-242

29. *"Ultimate Fighting Quotes and Quotations" accessed November 5, 2011, http://www.mmawild.com/ufc/quotes/*

30. *Terry E. Bush, "In it to win it," Fight! Magazine, May, 2010*

31. *Licia Avelar, "UFC Fighter Quarry Touts Revolutionary Spinal Surgery" December 25, 2010, accessed June 9, 2011, http://www.longislandpress.com/2010/12/25/ufc-fighter-quarry-touts-revolutionary-spinal-surgery/*

32. *"Denis Diderot Quotes" Think Exist, accessed November 6, 2011, http://thinkexist.com/quotation/only_passions-great_passions_can_elevate_the_soul/296764.html*

33. *"Best UFC Quote(s) from Pre/Post Fight," Inside MMA, accessed November 6, 2011, http://www.insidemma.com.au/index.php?option=com_kunena&Itemid=40&func=view&catid=7&id=189*

34. *"Dana White Quotes," Think Exist, accessed November 6, 2011, http://thinkexist.com/quotes/dana_white/2.html*

35. *Peter Drucker, "Michael Moncur's (Cynical) Quotations," accessed November 6, 2011, http://www.quotationspage.com/quote/26536.html*

36. *Jason Polley, "Kenny Florian and Marc Dellagrotte Go Their Separate Way," accessed April 5, 2010, http://fiveouncesofpain.com/2009/09/22/kenny-florian-and-marc-dellagrotte-go-their-separate-ways/*

37. *"John Updike Quotes", Think Exist, accessed November 6, 2011, http://thinkexist.com/quotation/a_leader_is_one_who-out_of_madness_or_goodness/261744.html*

38. *Mahatma Gandi, Quotations Book, accessed November 6, 2011, http://quotationsbook.com/quote/35436/*

39. *Chuck Mindenhall, "The Evolution of Kos," Fight! Magazine, September, 2010*

40. *"Tony Robbins Quotes," Brainy Quotes, accessed November 6, 2011, http://www.brainyquote.com/quotes/quotes/t/tonyrobbin126257.html*

41. *"Henry Ford Quotes," Think Exist, accessed November 6, 2011, http://thinkexist.com/quotation/failure_is_simply_the_opportunity_to_begin_again/13636.html*

42. *"Wilma Rudolph Quotes," Think Exist, accessed November 6, 2011, http://thinkexist.com/quotation/winning_is_great-sure-but_if_you_are_really_going/346114.html*

43. *"Napoleon Hill Quotes," Brainy Quote, accessed November 6, 2011, http://www.brainyquote.com/quotes/quotes/n/napoleonhi121336.html*

44. *"Malcolm S. Forbes Quotes," Think Exist, accessed November 6, 2011, http://thinkexist.com/quotation/victory_is_sweetest_when_you-ve_known_defeat/294745.html*

45. *Stephen J. Dubner, "Your U.F.C. Questions Answered," August 14, 2008, accessed April 7, 2010, http://www.freakonomics.com/2008/08/14/your-ufc-questions-answered/*

46. *Terry E. Bush, "In it to win it," Fight! Magazine, May, 2010*

47. *Clay Guida, "The Carpenter's Edge," Fight! Magazine June, 2010*

48. *"Tom Landry Quotes—Quotable Quotes," Good Reads, accessed November 6, 2011, http://www.goodreads.com/quotes/show/58284*

48. *"Author Unknown," Quotations About Effort, Quote Garden, accessed November 6, 2011, http://www.quotegarden.com/effort.html*

50. *"Vince Lombardi Quotes" Think Exist, accessed November 6, 2011, http://thinkexist.com/quotation/i_firmly_believe_that_any_man-s_finest_hour-the/173395.html*

51. *John Dryden, Quotations Book, accessed November 9, 2011, http://quotationsbook.com/quote/7844/*

52. *Author Unknown, Confidence Poems, Life with Confidence; A Positive Way of Thinking," accessed November 9, 2011, http://www.life-with-confidence.com/confidence-poem.html*

53. *Muhammad Ali, Muhammad Ali Quotes, Brainy Quote, accessed November 10, 2011, http://www.brainyquote.com/quotes/quotes/m/muhammadal136676.html*